THE GREATNESS PRINCIPLE

Have MORE ... confidence, support, balance & results

Jen Harwood

Motivational Speaker, Author & Business Coach

The Greatness Principle
Copyright © 2014 by Jennifer A. Harwood
ISBN: 978-0-9802811-2-5

Editor: Gaye Wilson, Gryphonworks, www.gryphonworks.com

Cover Design: Jen Picknell, Jenious Design Studio, www.jenious.com.au

Cover Photo: Angela Cushway, Willow Belle Portraits,
www.willowbelle.com.au

Interior Design: The Publishing Queen, www.thepublishingqueen.com

All rights reserved. No part of this publication may be reproduced, stored in a retrieval system or transmitted in any form or by any means electronic, mechanical, photocopying, recording, or otherwise without prior written permission from the publisher.

™ or ® denotes a Trademark or Registered Trademark owned by The Jenerator! Pty Ltd.

The author and publisher of this book do not make any claim or guarantee for any mental, emotional, physical, spiritual, relationship or financial result. All products, services and information provided by the author are for general education and entertainment purposes only. The information provided herein is in no way a substitute for medical advice, psychological diagnosis or advice, relationship counselling, business advice, financial advice or spiritual direction. In the event that you use any of the information contained in this book for yourself, the author and publisher assume no responsibility for your actions. The Jenerator! Pty Ltd accepts no responsibility or liability for any content, bibliographic references, quotes, artwork or works cited contained in this book.

Because of the dynamic nature of the internet, some web addresses contained in this book may have changed since publication and may no longer be valid.

Disclaimer: Case studies and examples used in this book are based on real events and people, but names and details in some cases have been changed to protect privacy.

Published by The Jenerator!
PO Box 161, Cremorne Junction
NSW, 2090 Australia
www.thejenerator.com

What people say about The Greatness Principle®

Since using the Greatness Wheel, my business interests have flourished, and my personal life rocks! It's simple enough for anyone to implement, and the results are immediate. I recommend this book to everyone, and particularly to the owners of small businesses who have been wondering what else they can do to take their business to the next level!

Liz Grant, What Your Customers Want

I have used the Greatness Principle® with my family to make them more aware of who is playing what roles within their lives. It has created some of the best conversations our family have had.

Kay V., Melbourne

As an independent consultant I am used to going it alone. The Greatness Principle® reminded me that to be effective as a sole operator I need to gather and nurture my Great8™. Many of these people have been there all along—I just didn't realise the important roles that they play for me both personally and professionally. I see them now as critical members of my organisation—they just get paid in lashings of appreciation rather than $$$.

Jen L., Geelong

When I heard Jen Harwood's Greatness Principle® I had a huge 'aha' moment. Suddenly I saw what I needed to do to take my business to the next level. Pure genius!

Nutritionist and Naturopath, Director Marshall Health

The Greatness Principle® reinforces the importance of engaging valuable people to provide assistance and support which will enable us to reach our true potential in our business and life. I found the concept inspiring, engaging and refreshingly honest. Above all, it left me in no doubt there is still much to learn; also the advantages of networking with positive people who will guide us in our journey to achieve success.

Elaine Munro, Owner East Geelong Newsagency, Geelong East Post Office, Coffee on Garden and Tech Revive

I've found Jen to be one of the most prolific and practical thought leaders I have ever had the pleasure to meet. She is in that rare category of business advisers who can explain and express business concepts while possessing the gift of developing practical and implementable programs to make them happen, to achieve results and desired outcomes. Jen continues to inspire others through her messages, her programs and her personality. She is a motivating communicator, value creator and, most importantly, a true Jenerator of possibility and potential.

Iggy Pintado, General Manager, Australian Institute of Company Directors

THE GIFT OF GREATNESS

Dear _____

You are a very special person to me and I just wanted to tell you that.

My life has had many challenges and turns, and you have been there, by my side, supporting me. *Thank you!*

Your involvement in my life has made me so happy, confident and courageous. *Thank you!*

Knowing I had your support, encouragement, dose of reality, strategies and ideas to make my life happen has kept me in better balance. Everything works better now. *Thank you!*

Your faith, belief and commitment to me, my life and dreams is priceless. *Thank you!*

I am so very grateful for every conversation, knowing glance, question of clarification, emotional outburst, ideas brainstorm, celebration and personal moments that we have shared together. *Thank you!*

The Great8 Investor you have been for me is _____

Thank you for being your fabulous self and causing my world to be great.

Gratefully yours,

Dedication

This book is dedicated to all the lonely leaders in business, family and our community who are committed to making a difference.

You are not alone any more and the time for you to realise GREATNESS is now!

Letter from the author

Too many times we see others fail in business and say, 'oh what a shame they failed. It was a great business, pity the people who ran it weren't'. Over the last decade of working with over a thousand business owners, I have come to realise that the people whose businesses had failed weren't bad people at all. In fact, they weren't stupid or lazy, as many would think would be the case when it comes to failure. What they all had in common was that they all had, for various reasons, disconnected from the people who supported them and therefore were experiencing a massive breakdown in their business.

When I say breakdown, the most common breakdowns for business owners are:

Physical—heart attack, stroke, ulcers, cancer, being grossly overweight or anorexic

Financial—massive debt, serious overspending, bankruptcy

Mental—depression, social isolation, withdrawal from family/community

Letter from the author

Emotional—anxiety, mood disorders, rage outbursts, stress-related conditions

Spiritual—suicide, addictions: alcohol, drugs, sex addictions, crime

Now, I'm not a doctor, scientist, psychologist or therapist of any kind. I am a business expert and what I have witnessed in 1100 individual business owners I have worked with intensively over the last 15 years is this … all of the owners whose business was failing experienced some or all of the breakdowns I've mentioned above, and more.

Note: This is not the platform to discuss the clinical diagnosis of the 'cause' of how depression, anxiety, mood disorders, heart attacks, cancer and ulcers occur. Also I am not saying that being in business causes cancer or depression or heart attacks or anything of that nature. Consider that all of the breakdowns mentioned are 'red flags' indicating that you are on a path to business or personal failure. They are an opportunity for you to STOP and review your position immediately and change direction AWAY from failure.

I've written this book for four reasons:

1. To let my clients and other business owners know what they need to do to ensure their business, lives and families are GREAT;

2. To let everyone else know that they are equally responsible to NOTICE when someone is in breakdown and how to support them build their greatness back up. I believe the time has come for our society to realise that we are all connected, we are all responsible for everyone winning the game of life, and now there is an easy system for people to implement to give and receive support;

3. My wish is that The Greatness Principle® is shared and embraced by everyone so that we can all work together to run great businesses, grow great people, families and communities, and to BE GREAT;

4. My last reason is to serve humanity. This book is based on my own observations and work to support and empower leaders to be great and have great results. I start the conversation of the Greatness Principle® and invite/challenge other experts from other disciplines, universities and business schools to take this concept on and scientifically prove it, and then work it into how we teach our children, our business leaders and our communities to live, engage and thrive.

Jen Harwood

Disclaimer

This book offers ideas and strategies that may support people be successful and have a great life. If the reader is experiencing violence, force, domination, blackmail, bribery, any law-breaking activities or is under the advice and care of medical professionals such as psychologists, counsellors, doctors or specialists, please seek professional advice before adopting and implementing these ideas into your life or business.

This book has come from over 15 years of personal work I have done coaching and consulting to business owners and their families. I have worked with over one thousand businesses and spoken with many thousands of people in seminars and workshops to formulate the Greatness Principle® Concept. Hence, these strategies and points of view are my own and from my own work. I offer the Greatness Principle® as a contribution for the reader in the following ways:

- To consider how successful and balanced each of the areas of your life are and what to do about it;
- As a review of the current active relationships in your life and to see if they are serving you;
- To provide strategies and ideas on how to support others in your life, businesses and community in a way you may not have considered before.

Contents

Dedication vii
Letter from the author ix
Disclaimer xiii
Contents xv

Chapter 1: Why is Greatness important today? 1
    The Greatness fantasy 2
    Why the Greats are great! 5
    Why focus on Greatness now? 6

Chapter 2: What do great leaders need? 9
    1. Vision 9
    2. Personal awareness 22
    3. Character 23
    4. Having a personal support team 27
    Great leaders also need vulnerability 30

Chapter 3: Isolation doesn't work 33
    The cost of isolation 37
    Breakdown and the reality check 38
    Things people say when they are isolated 39

Chapter 4: The Greatness Principle® 41
    Where did it come from? 41
    Creating the Greatness Wheel 53
    The Greatness Wheel: Your Great8™ 54
    The Great8™ life ring analogy 55

Contents

Chapter 5: The Greatness Investor roles ... 59
Enthusiast: optimism, energy, possibility ... 61
- How to relate to the Enthusiast ... 62
- How to be the Enthusiast ... 62
- Investor warning ... 63

Sage: authenticity, wisdom, freedom ... 64
- How to relate to the Sage ... 65
- How to be the Sage ... 65
- Investor warning ... 66

Motivator: commitment, action, accountability ... 67
- How to relate to the Motivator ... 68
- How to be the Motivator ... 68
- Investor warning ... 69

Bystander: interest, information, perspective ... 70
- How to relate to the Bystander ... 71
- How to be the Bystander ... 72
- Investor warning ... 72

Anchor: belief, confidence, pride ... 73
- How to relate to the Anchor ... 74
- How to be the Anchor ... 74
- Investor warning ... 75

Grounder: realist, sceptic, practical ... 76
- How to relate to the Grounder ... 77
- How to be the Grounder ... 77
- Investor warning ... 78

Catalyst: incitement, challenge, growth ... 79
- How to relate to the Catalyst ... 80
- How be the Catalyst ... 81
- Investor warning ... 81

Scholar: ideas, intellect, consequences ... 83
- How to relate to the Scholar ... 84
- How to be the Scholar ... 84
- Investor warning ... 85

Corrective Feedback: why it is important for Greatness ... 86
Your Investors have your best interests at heart ... 87
- Enthusiast ... 87
- Sage ... 87
- Motivator ... 88
- Bystander ... 88
- Anchor ... 89
- Grounder ... 89
- Catalyst (negative angle) ... 90
- Catalyst (positive angle) ... 90

Scholar 91
What do the Great8™ get from being involved? 91

Chapter 6: The First Investor™ 97
Get clear on the facts 99
Clean up the past 101
Tell the truth 101
Why Bother?—the assassin of Greatness................................... 102
Boundary management 105
How to be the First Investor™ to yourself 108
Investor warning... 109

Chapter 7: Greatness Principle® rules...................................... 111
1. Choose one Domain at a time... 111
2. The Great8™ must be alive... 116
3. Great8™ Investors must wait to be asked for corrective feedback to achieve maximum effect 117
4. You must have one person in one role only........................ 118
5. You don't need to know about the Greatness Principle® for it to work 119
6. The Substitute Investor 121
7. The Cloaked Investor™... 122
8. Growth: fill your wheel, then double it, then move on 127
How do you know that your Great8™ have your back? 128

Chapter 8: The great breakdown... 133
How to rebuild your Greatness Wheel 143
What if you have a full wheel and the Great8™ you have aren't good? 147

Chapter 9: Wheel dynamics 151
Free Spirits 152
Greatness strategy for Free Spirits 153
The Turbo Chargers 154
Greatness strategy for Turbo Chargers 155
The Plodders.. 156
Greatness strategy for Plodders 157
Gauntlet Runners... 158
Greatness strategy for Gauntlet Runners............................ 160
The Drama Makers 161
Greatness strategies for Drama Makers............................... 163

Chapter 10: How to bring a Great8™ Investor into your wheel 169
Known Investor... 169

Contents

    Unknown Investor 170
    The Benefits of groups 171
        Group support can be easier than one-on-one 171
        Groups are a great place where you can invest in others 174

Chapter 11: Case studies 175
    1. Business 175
        How a business breaks down 'overnight' 175
    2. Business leadership 178
        How to rebuild a great business 178
    3. Career 184
        Broke, drunk and depressed 184
    4. Spiritual enlightenment 188
        The role of God or a higher power in the greatness 188
    5. Living responsibly 192
        It's not about ME anymore 192

After thoughts 197

An Invitation 199
    Further Training and Courses in the Greatness Principle® 199
        Level 1: The Great Life (2 days) 199
        Level 2: The Great Leader (2 days) 200
        The Greatness Principle® Accredited
        Facilitators Program (3 Days) 200
    The Greatness Principle® Coaching Programs 201
    The Greatness Principle® Products 201
        Greatness Cards 201
        Greatness Principle® T-Shirts 202
        Greatness Party Pack 203

Who is Jen Harwood? 205

Acknowledgements 207

Greatness Wheel templates 211

Chapter 1

Why is Greatness important today?

Have you ever heard the saying 'Behind every great man, there is a great woman', or vice versa? It has many different connotations depending on your point of view. The position I take on this quote is that to create a GREAT person (in this case a man), there will be just one person (in this case a woman) behind him, investing in him to make him great.

Now, think about that situation for just a minute. How much pressure is on the supporter to help 'turn out' the success for the other? It also means that she has to give up her life's mission to focus on him and together they create his desired result. That may have worked in the past, as the primary gender values and expectations were different for past generations. However, if you look at recent times, the really GREAT people in the world in any arena (eg. business, sport, politics, science, fashion, media, technology) have more than just ONE person behind them investing in them and, most importantly, NONE of the support people have to give up their life's mission to support the GREAT person.

Chapter 1

The simplest example to use would be some of history's greatest top seed tennis stars like Steffi Graf and Roger Federer. Picture it: at the Grand Slam finals, these GREAT tennis stars have in the stadium right next to the court a private box for their supporters. Now, if the 'Great Man/Great Woman' quote were true, there would be only one seat in the private box for the 'wife/husband/partner' of the player.

In fact these private boxes have at least eight seats in them, and guess who's there ... husband/wife, mum/dad, brother/sister, tennis coach, physiotherapist, life partner, best friend, business manager, corporate sponsor representative etc. ALL of these people invest in the GREAT player. They contribute specific qualities and points of view that have caused the tennis player to BE GREAT, and these people are GREAT in their own right, as they too have created their own personal support network. Success creates success. It makes sense that a GREAT Champion's support people have their own balanced support too.

Greatness is all about creating sustainable success. Having an individual foundation of strength and perspective ensures that emotional, physical, spiritual and mental states are balanced. This allows the individual to have good health, emotional stability, mental clarity and a healthy spirit. When you have these four areas in balance, you make great choices and decisions and take massive action because your confidence is high and you are really truly supported.

The Greatness fantasy

Many times a day others will ask us how we are, how's business? How's the family? How's your day? And our automatic response is usually 'Yeah, great!'

It's easy to get caught up in the fantasy of being great and having a great business. In my experience in working with over 1100 business owners and leaders, they have all actually experienced moments or periods of time being GREAT in projects, teams, personal achievements, sports, careers and other circumstances. They know themselves through the past as a success, a winner and someone who is capable of great things. So off they go, with full confidence and expectation that they can replicate their great success in a new domain in their life, career or business.

In fact, their self-confidence, bordering on unconscious arrogance, causes them to believe that the reason the past success happened was due to them being GREAT! Ah, the trap has silently sprung and they are caught in a self-fulfilling future of failure, as this time they will not be open or willing to create and work the Greatness Principle® they naturally and unconsciously used last time.

What's interesting is that in nearly all of my client's experiences, in their previous endeavours, when their venture was so important for reasons beyond themselves, they quickly realised that they didn't know enough, or didn't have the resources they needed, and identified others who could make the venture happen WITH THEM. That allowed a free flow of contributions in ideas, advice, resources, finance, and equipment: whatever was needed to ensure the venture worked. You see, they were letting the venture work through them for others (greatness) instead of working hard at a venture so they could make a contribution and take the credit for it, or prove they did it!

Yes, commonness, mediocrity, averageness … everyone wants to prove themselves or take credit for outcomes and results. That's our ego's demand and a natural want in the experience of being human. To have greatness in your life, you must be committed to building your own character and resilience, to not making everything about yourself, to working in collaboration with others and realising the simple and powerful truth, which is … **your life matters, your life affects others and it's your responsibility (not anyone else's) to bring greatness to every aspect of your life, no matter what the circumstances.**

Chapter 1

At present, the world really isn't geared to this principle. Media, popular culture and peer pressure cause us all to … FOCUS on SELF! Look good, say good things, be a good person, be successful, get out there and make it happen, be seen to be making a difference and the result of doing all of that is that you will have a GREAT life. Rubbish. If you do all of that you'll get only one result … you will be SEEN to be having a great life, but your life will all be about you PROVING you have a great life, and that, in my opinion, is pretty mediocre, ordinary and a lot of hard work!

The people who have a GREAT life and GREAT businesses have their heads focussed on what is important in their lives (not focussed on others and seeking recognition from others). They have strong, deep relationships that they regularly invest in and they do not feel the need to prove anything to anyone! They have a strong sense of character about who they are for themselves, their family, their business and their community. They are leaders in their life and they understand that who they are and what they do affects others, and they take a genuine responsibility for that. Think about your community, your industry or an area of your life. You know the GREAT people. You've seen them. You know they're not on a proving/look good mission that could fall over in a heartbeat. They have a way about them that's calmer, even if what they are dealing with at the time is stressful and a lot to bear. They consider, they reflect, they have a way with people that engages rather than repels. Life works for these people and it keeps getting better. Why? They see a bigger future than the immediate here and now and they know they must engage others in their life to contribute to the outcome.

What's wonderful about this way of living and being is that anyone can do it, and you can too. What's even more exciting is that you can start from anywhere: from being financially bankrupt; isolated from all your friends due to feuds and disagreements, divorce or separation; life-changing illness that's turned your life into something completely different; moving house, state or country; from being deep in a drug addiction or even starting from a prison cell. The first thing you

MUST do, is OWN the mess you are in. All of it. The good, the bad and especially the UGLY. You are in a place in your life that doesn't work, isn't working, or is not as great as it could be, and the only person responsible for it … IS YOU and you need and must ask for support to sort it all out. That's a very exciting place to be.

Why the Greats are great!

Who are the greatest people in history? Both men and women, you can find them everywhere in all aspects of human endeavour. They have been studied and examined. We get inspired by their quotes, their statements and their results, yet the area that I believe is the 'invisible success factor' to their greatness is:

1. The combination and quality of people that they have chosen to surround themselves with; AND
2. Their overall approach to relationships.

Let's list a few people who are globally well known: Winston Churchill, Oprah, Abraham Lincoln, Arianna Huffington, Barack Obama, Mother Theresa, Mahatma Gandhi, Princess Diana, Nelson Mandela, Margaret Thatcher.

Society, as a whole, takes these people and lifts them up for their greatness and applies it to the totality of their life. If they are living, they have the pressure to live up to that 'greatness standard' in every area of their life … for the rest of their life. If they have died, they are immortalised forever for their great glorious moments and contribution. Where does that leave the rest of us? Most people don't acknowledge their greatness as they don't see themselves to be in the same league. Is that true for you?

It's important to remember that 'The Greats' were and are human and for many of them they weren't great in all areas of their lives. They had their moments in life where they weren't great, for example, Elvis

Presley, Michael Jackson, Marilyn Monroe, Greg Norman and Tiger Woods. Even as you read these 'great' names, you know they had many non-great moments, just like all of us.

Similarly, if you know your history, Winston Churchill wasn't a great sleeper and caused friction with his allies in World War II, Abraham Lincoln was often indecisive, Mother Theresa flew first class despite her vows of poverty, and Princess Diana didn't have a great marriage and suffered from eating disorders.

What I've found in coaching thousands of people over the last 15 years is that we are all great at something, and the more we can embrace that something, the greater value we are to others. Greatness comes about by being true to your nature and abilities, having the courage to 'go deep in your chosen domain of life', and relying and TRUSTING others to fill in the gaps where you are not so great.

Why focus on Greatness now?

Similarly, on a more everyday level, from my own observation, what is common between successful business owners, couples who have been married for more than 20 years, and community organisations that successfully and consistently raise funding for their work is that they don't take on new friends/partners or supporters quickly. They stand back and assess the potential person and usually assess informally if the person matches their values, style of thinking and way of being. If the prospect passes the test, something wonderful happens.

When the prospect passes the test and there is a perceived fit, the leader then commits to work with the prospect for the long term. They are interested in years of association / friendship / business venture for more than five years at least. They expect long-term investment from themselves and also from the new person they have brought into their world.

Also, they know what it takes to have a long-term relationship:

1. Compatible partner choice (similar and/or appropriate views, values and character);
2. Willing to communicate no matter the circumstances;
3. Complete commitment to the joint outcome;
4. Great boundary and expectation management;
5. Having the other's best interests in focus when making decisions, choices and taking action, a duty of care.

When two people have this going on between them, they can work together and create GREAT outcomes.

Now for some people, this is a no brainer. However, for a lot of people today, this is a bit strange and new. Over the last 50 years we have been conditioned to be a disposable society. We use and discard packaging, food, cars, furniture, digital equipment and now people. Today, if a person doesn't agree with us, annoys us or hurts us, even a little bit, we tend to cut them off, remove them from our life and find someone else. We do that in business with joint partners, co-owners, staff and suppliers. We do that in marriages. We do that with close and extended family and also with friends. We do that with community groups, social ventures and even online in social media.

The GREATS of the world don't discard people and relationships quickly. They may manoeuvre or manage difficult relationships and eventually end them, however they work at the relationship, they give it space, time and patience and they also appreciate its benefits and opportunities without fast negative judgement or discard. Great people who are experiencing greatness in any domain of life value people.

So, it's time to start paying attention to the secret of success that no-one talks about. It's what I call…

Chapter 1

The Greatness Principle®.

No-one ever becomes great and stays great all by themselves!

It is clear from all the work I have done with leaders of small businesses that the leader is the barometer of how healthy and balanced the business, family or organisation is. When the leader is balanced and centred, great decisions, delegation and accountability are in place. When the leader is out of balance, the whole business / family / organisation wobbles, tips and eventually falls over. Leaders need to be steady and balanced in themselves to make great decisions for all involved. Leaders need support in identifying where they are unsupported and out of balance and where they can focus energy and attention to regain composure and control.

> *Men of character are the conscience of the society to which they belong.*
> **~ Ralph Waldo Emerson**

Chapter 2

What do great leaders need?

There are four key elements to leadership in any domain of life (business / career / family / health / wealth / community etc.) that are essential for greatness. These are vision, personal awareness, character and a support team. Think of these four elements as legs on a table. A stable table has four solid legs and it won't fall or tip over. It can also bear a lot of weight and burden, as it is solid and balanced. We want to see every leader working on the four elements of great leadership all the time. As these elements in our lives become stronger, equally our lives and results get better.

1. Vision

If you can imagine it, you can achieve it
If you can dream it, you can become it.
~ William Arthur Ward

Chapter 2

Vision is essential for Greatness. If you don't have something to strive for, something to work towards, you are wandering along and have nothing to channel your energy, drive and focus. Your vision is the future world that you want to create and that you are prepared to put all your focus, energy, drive, funds, and attention into creating. You're passionate about it and you stand solid on it.

Your vision must be something that totally engages, inspires and motivates you as YOU are going to be the champion for the vision and you will need to be able to stand the test of time, endure all the distractions, challenges and setbacks to then keep pushing forward to realise the vision.

Your vision/future picture needs to be clear and defined. The steps on how to create the vision in the first place won't necessarily be clear and that's okay. Just like JFK declared the following vision in 1961:

> *'I believe that this nation should commit itself to achieving the goal, before this decade is out, of landing a man on the moon and returning him safely to the earth.'*
> **~ John F. Kennedy, Man on the Moon Speech,
> Joint Session of Congress 25th May, 1961**

This vision was definitely a commitment to the future, one to which JFK and his administration would commit time, money, resources, focus and people to make the vision happen. JFK's vision commanded commitment from the team as well as support and encouragement from the country and the world. Great visions tap into personal dreams and dance in possibility and potential. They are more than goals and as such have an invisible power that attracts energy, focus and success.

So, as a leader in your business and/or your career and/or your family and personal life, what are your dreams and vision for your business, your life or a specific domain in your life? What is it that you MUST achieve to make your time here on earth worthwhile?

If you have poor results in your business, family or life, the first place to look at is your current vision for that area. When we have a compelling vision that we are working towards, we have a big enough reason to get out of bed. This is what gets us to do the little bit extra after hours, before work, in between phone calls, to push though the emergencies of life and stay on track to keep moving towards the vision.

The best way I've found to create a vision is to remove yourself from normal circumstances and daily activities and take yourself to an environment that is very like your vision, or if that's not possible because your vision doesn't exist on the planet yet, go somewhere that allows you to dream, think and wander in your mind and heart for a few hours, ideally a few days. Once you get the picture, or the words or the feelings of what you would really like to have, capture it.

There are several ways to capture your vision. The easiest way is to draw a picture, a vision board. It doesn't have to be an award-winning drawing, it just needs to have the elements of what you want to create and have tangible specifics on the outcomes you want to achieve. To be able to draw such a picture, it's helpful to list all the outcomes/results for the vision and even give the vision a title. When we call the overall vision a name or give it a phrase that motivates and energises us, it has more power. For example:

Chapter 2

Business
Turnover $20 million
Profit $5 million
Location: Office 10 mins from home
Staff: 10, cohesive team
My time: part-time or out of day-to-day
Vision = Business Freedom

Family
Happy spouse / partner
Children happy and fully supported
Home: safe, nurturing, fun
Friends: involved and active in our family
Strong sibling and cousin connections
Vision = Strong Happy Family

Career
Income $200k
Saving 20–50%
Travelling to four countries per year
Progression to being leader of the team
Recognition by peers or industry
Vision = Industry Expert

Health
Body fat down to 10%
Run the local marathon in under three hours
Pain- and illness-free
Can run and play with my children
Wear beautiful clothes and feel amazing
Vision = Hot, Fit and Sexy

Examples of vision boards are on the next few pages. As you can see, they can be visually appealing and they represent the person's desired emotional experience and tangible outcome.

What do great leaders need?

Domain: Holiday—this family dreamed of going to Europe for six weeks. They did it. (Jennifer Franklin Bell)

Chapter 2

Domain: Money and Me Vision
(Clare Fountain)

Domain: Business Vision
(Clare Fountain)

What do great leaders need?

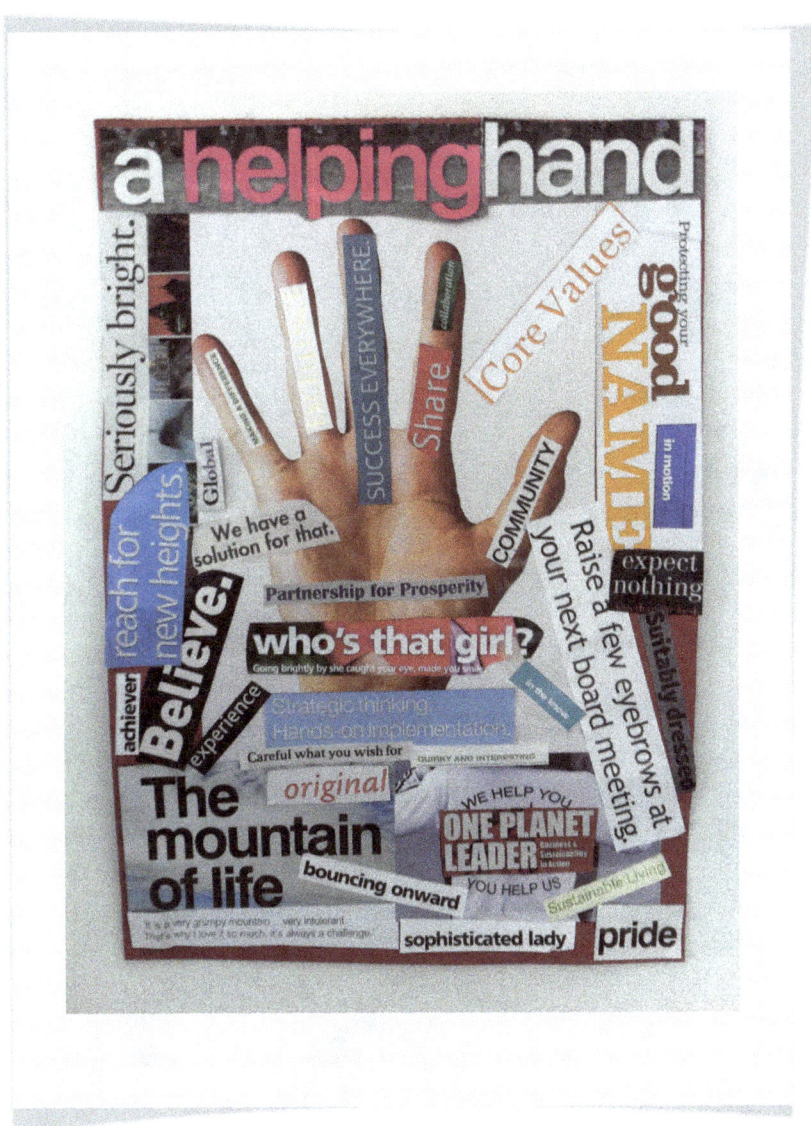

Domain: Personal Vision
(Clare Fountain)

Chapter 2

*Domain: Wellbeing—How I would experience life, health and family
(Jen Picknell)*

*Domain: Business—Book, Studio and Gallery
(Jenious Design Studios)*

What do great leaders need?

Domain: Friendship and Love
(used with permission: the creator asked to be anonymous)

Chapter 2

Domain: My Future
(Grace, aged 14 years)

What do great leaders need?

Domain: Financial Freedom (Jen Harwood)

Domain: Creating Family—find a husband, make a home, have a baby! (Jen Harwood)

Chapter 2

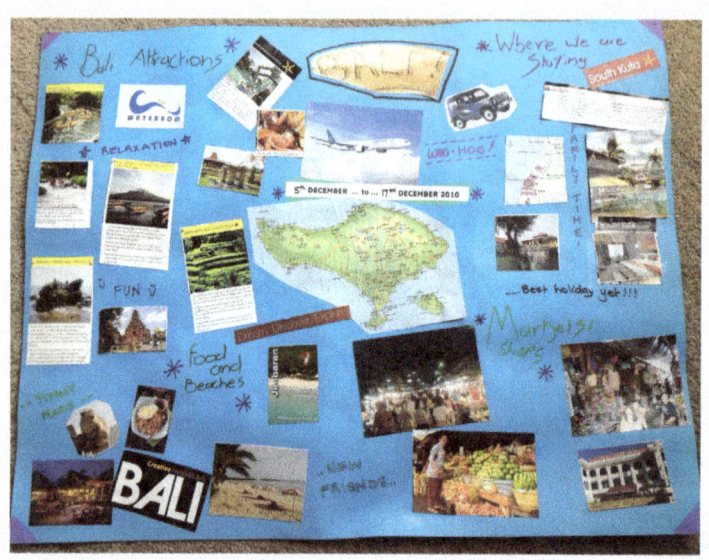

*Domain: New Beginnings for Family Vision Board
(Marie Farrugia)*

Marie's Story

Six months after I had my mastectomy (December 2009), our family created this vision board about a holiday we wanted to have. There seemed to be no way we could afford this because I wasn't working and medical bills had sucked up any savings (not to mention the credit cards were maxed out).

However, I urged my husband and son to do this project together as a 'let's see what we can create' thing. I have been using vision boards for many years, love them, but they had never made one. So off they went and made this fun one up. I added a few words around the place to keep the vibrations up.

> Outcome: We didn't book until about August 2010 after I received a call for some training to be done: a big contract that made us feel secure enough to purchase our first overseas holiday.
>
> Of course we had a blast! My son was impressed with the Balinese customer service and friendliness as well as the new culture and food he was introduced to. It was one of the best things we've done as a family.

Now, when you have created this vision, put it up on the wall where you can see it daily and keep a copy of it (a smaller printed version) in your wallet. Look at it, study it and allow yourself to visit that place and imagine that it is real and happening. The more you visit this vision, feel it and imagine it real, the better. The subconscious mind is a very powerful tool when it comes to creating results. As you daydream and imagine your vision, your subconscious mind, which is the background filter to the millions of bits of daily information your mind receives, will begin to notice more items, opportunities and situations that are related to the vision you want and you will 'see' them. If your vision hadn't been created and focussed on, you may not have noticed or even seen opportunities or little things that you really might have benefited from.

It's okay to have a list of things you want to achieve on a piece of paper. The key is to read it daily and take a few minutes to imagine it being real, and imagine yourself having that list of things. In my experience and from watching clients achieve great results, the more active you are in imagining, daydreaming and giving time to feel it, see it and 'play the tape', the more focussed you become.

2. Personal awareness

Great leaders have a good idea of who they are (their strengths and weaknesses) and the IMPACT they create on others. If you are going to be GREAT at anything, you've got to understand yourself at this basic level. Knowing yourself will achieve a few things.

1. You are able to work and develop your strengths.
2. You are able to manage your weaknesses. Now, don't tell me you don't have any weaknesses (things you're not very good at or things you don't care too much about). Everyone has them, so it's best that you work out what yours are so you can identify people, services and tools to manage them. None of us are perfect and able to do and manage everything all the time. We are human to have strengths and weaknesses. I believe it's all part of life's design, as we MUST work with others to grow, learn, create and live a happy, fulfilling life.
3. When you know yourself, you react less. When you react less, you have less drama. When you have less drama, you have the ability to do and create more, you don't have as much distraction and, most importantly, you are less emotional and more balanced.

There are plenty of personal development programs all over the world. You can go to week-long conferences and retreats, one-day intensives or even venture on year-long personal discovery programs. There are millions of books, courses, experts, counsellors, life coaches and the like that will support you to understand who you are. There are also multitudes of personality and character evaluation tools such as DISC®, MBTI® and GPTP®, and I encourage you to use them. Figure yourself out and then KEEP MOVING. I believe too many people have been caught up in the personal development industry and they live in the world of constantly improving themselves. At the end of the day, the best way to be GREAT is to get out into the world and learn about yourself through working with others.

So do a self-audit on your strengths, weaknesses and current skills and abilities. There is no right or wrong here. It is about being aware of what you are currently made up of, knowing that, over time, this list can and will change, depending on what your vision is and the choices and decisions you make moving forward in life.

Exercise for you to complete

Use the table below to note your current strengths, weaknesses, skills and abilities. Revisit the list at least twice a year.

Strengths	Weaknesses	Skills	Abilities

3. Character

Character is the mental and moral qualities distinctive to an individual. Simply put, your character is the sum of the little things you do on a consistent basis that define and shape you. Your character is a reflection of your discipline in any domain in your life.

For example, if you lack character and have no discipline with regards to food, health and wellbeing, you will be fat, sluggish and sick. If you lack character in your business, you will have inconsistent sales, unreliable people, problems with customers, and a bumpy, unpredictable, cash flow and turnover of people. Lack of character = lack of power.

Your character defines the way you react to circumstances. The only way to get power into your life, in any domain, is to re-define who you are going to BE with respect to your new vision and then BE it—no

Chapter 2

matter what: no matter the circumstances, barriers, distractions, interruptions, deviations, others' points of view or opinions. The truest way to build your character is to create your new set of rules about your vision and your life and then deliver on that for yourself. You don't do it to prove to anyone else that you can, you do it because … you promised yourself.

When you have strong character, you hold yourself accountable to be, do and have what you said you wanted and who you said you'd be to yourself! It's about honouring yourself and doing what is right for you and others.

This is a very powerful place to be. Every leader MUST consider their character and who they are being and who they need to be to create the vision and results they want. What's also interesting is that as you stand strong in character, other people will start aligning themselves to you and start to think, act and behave in the same way. You resonate a way of being that is not only attractive, it is infectious, and others start to adapt and replicate your commitments, actions, values and virtues in the domain with which you are associated. Leaders cause greatness when they accept that they are great and daily reinforce and strengthen their character.

The most global example of this that I can highlight is Disneyland. There are a number of them now in the world. Walt Disney had a vision. It was:

A place where children and parents could have fun together.

He dreamed of a 'magical park'.

The vision of Walt Disney had two profound effects. The first was that he didn't give up on his vision of building the park. There were many setbacks and knockbacks, problems and challenges that Walt had to deal with, including a lack of funding. In the end, the park opened. However, that didn't go smoothly either. The asphalt was still steaming and not fully set on the day of opening because it was only laid the night before. There were thousands of counterfeit tickets made for the opening and people came into the park uninvited. Walt stood firm on his vision and didn't let the 'little' things stop him or cloud the reality that his vision was here and building in reality every day.

The other aspect of Walt Disney, and the character of who he was as a person, was deeply embedded in Disney theme parks, the staff and the whole experience of going to Disneyland. I am sure that, if you asked many of the staff who worked at Disneyland over the years, they would say their lives and outlook changed to be even more positive, open and creative AND they had more fun. Many of them probably brought their family to the park too.

When you immerse yourself in a culture (the collective character of a group), that culture embeds into the people who are part of it, and they in turn do more of it, and the character of the business and the culture of the community becomes even stronger. What's your character? How is it showing up in your business? How is that affecting your staff, your clients and your suppliers? Is your business a fun, happy, wonderful place for everyone to work and create or is it hard, frustrating, negative, distrusting, and staff and customers are interacting, not connecting?

You are the leader. It's all a reflection of YOU!

To be a GREAT leader in business, you need to know what your moral code is and what your rules of doing business are. Are you prepared to stick by your code and rules even when there is a deal that doesn't quite fit, a customer who's demanding a refund, or when a competitor outsmarts your marketing? Are you at the mercy of circumstances and situations, or are you greater than that?

If you are going to be a GREAT spouse or life partner, what are your moral code and rules for relationships and loving? Are you prepared to stick by your code and rules even when they have cheated on you, committed a crime, destroyed something you own or they get an illness that makes them completely dependent on you for the rest of your life? Who are you going to be in those moments, day by day, year by year?

If you are going to be a GREAT parent to your children, what are your moral code and rules of living and interacting with other people and loving your children? Are you prepared to stick to them when your child has a meltdown at 5 pm outside a shop with half a dozen people watching you and potentially judging you? Who are you going to be when someone else is being cruel or nasty to your child? Are you prepared to stand up and act on your moral code and rules for relating in those moments?

Life has its ups and downs and we all will come up against challenge. It's essential for growth and development. Challenge actually causes character to grow. It's the challenges and resistance in life that build emotional, mental, physical and spiritual character. The easy times must not be overlooked as that is where we must be mindful and diligent to keep good habits, thoughts and actions in place. If we become complacent, all the work we did in a hard time in our life is lost because we've been lazy, over-indulgent, loose on boundaries and forgetful.

I know I've been like that. Early on in my career, I was earning a lot of money and I spent it and didn't save any. I went out every night to dinner with different friends and family, took regular holidays and had a luxurious life. I didn't manage my money well because I thought I'd have my job forever and all would be good. I was living in the moment and I hadn't developed my character or awareness around money at all. So when I decided to leave my job (because I was bored), I thought everything would be okay as I always earned well. So I started my own business. I got clients and lots of work, however my character, discipline and habits around money were very under-developed and so, within 18 months of being in business, I had generated a business turnover of $180,000 in consulting fees with a yearly profit of $10,000, but had also created $70,000 in personal debt on five different credit cards. My previous seven years of daily decisions and choices around money were not serving me in my business. I had to assess the situation and choose an option—bankruptcy or pay back the debt and learn how to manage and respect money. I chose the latter.

It took me almost five years to pay it all off and start rebuilding. My character in the domain of money got stronger and also, as I made more money, I was better managing it, investing it and spending it. The people I was spending time with also had stronger characters and values around money. If you have experienced something like this, good. I hope you have stepped up and started to work on your character. On the other hand, if you are in a situation with money, health, relationships or business that is really bad and not working, you need to get real now and start to do something about it. You have a weak character and weak values in that area and it is VITAL that you start to develop it NOW. You are going to need support from other people to do this—building character when you are on your own or not talking to people is pretty hard and slow going to create change.

4. Having a personal support team

Essentially that is what this book is all about. As a leader, you need a team of people that you can lean on who share the same values and virtues and ideally have a strong character in the domain on which you are focussed.

For example, if you were looking to grow your business turnover from $2 million to $20 million per year, then you would need to start looking for people who are doing $20 million or better. They have demonstrated they have the character to grow and lead a business of that size and influence. They view business problems and challenges differently than $2-million-dollar businesses and start-ups. They have also developed their character as they've been through the tough times, the resistance and challenge that have taught them and created new disciplines, moral codes and rules of working. These are excellent people to share time with and be around. Remember, strong character attracts people and when in a group, people start to change, adapt and adopt to the strongest character traits of the group.

Another example of this would be on the home front. If your five-year marriage is shaky and about to fall apart, you need to look for people who have been married for 15–20 years who have demonstrated their character, moral code and rules of relating and loving that have proven to be effective for long-term relationships. These are the people you want to start talking to and being with. Their way of viewing their long-term relationship and the strategies, rules and character on how to do that will be so much different to people struggling with being married for only 4–5 years.

The other key element to building your support team is that you must qualify that all the support team members are 'invested' in YOU, that they have YOUR best interests at heart. Let me explain. Investors of any currency, be it money, gold, time, or resources, are looking for 'quality investments' that value their contribution and ultimately give them a 'return' on their investment. The people in your support team are effectively INVESTORS in YOU! They value YOU and they believe through their experience of you and your character that you are worth investing in. The other part of their support relationship with you is that they also believe that they are going to get some form of return on their investment. Now before you freak out, thinking this is all about money—it's not. Greatness is an amazing experience. You can feel it at world-class performances in any domain. For example:

The best ballerina in the world doing an entrechat in Swan Lake
Tiger Woods winning the Masters Tournament for the fourth time
Michael Schumacher winning the Formula One Grand Prix more times than anyone else
Roger Federer winning the Grand Slam 17 times
The first landing on the moon in 1969—a huge team effort
Nelson Mandela becoming President of South Africa

When an individual or group is performing at a world-class A grade level, there is an energy, an intensity, a simplicity and magnified beauty of what is being done and how it's being experienced by the doer and the watcher that's potent and infectious. When we watch or are involved in something like that, we feel good. We get inspired, we feel motivated and start taking action and sometimes even make new choices, visions and dreams. For a moment, we stop focussing on our woes, our dramas and our challenges, and dance in the possibilities and bask in the greatness that is before us and around us. As my mother Cath would have said … it's Magic!

The support team you want in your life experiences this with YOU. They will invest in YOU because either through you or with you, they touch greatness. That is a very valuable asset for anyone.

So, with that in mind, the stronger the character, experience and wisdom qualities you want in your personal support team, the better and stronger you have to become. You want to make yourself worthy, valuable and the best quality human being you can be, remembering that it takes a lifetime to develop and you can work on yourself all the time. Therefore it's very important to understand that the other three elements (Vision, Personal Awareness and Character) are vital to great leadership and attracting and keeping solid support. Your personal support team WON'T be strong and solid if you are not clear about where you are going, or if you don't understand the impact you have on others and/or you are not being true to yourself.

So these are the four legs of the Great Leader Table. There is one more thing that enhances greatness, and that is vulnerability. Consider it the table top: a big, wide surface that is the basis for building long-term relationships.

Chapter 2

Great leaders also need vulnerability

When you have people who are committed and invested in you, you must learn to TRUST them if you are going to build that relationship for the long term. For many people, that can be incredibly confronting and scary and, believe me, I know there are many things that we don't want to share, talk about, acknowledge or take responsibility for. That's normal and natural. We all have secrets and things we're embarrassed by or ashamed about or feel guilty for. This is part of being human and, as hard as it may seem, to be a great leader in any area of your life—business, family, community—you are going to have to be vulnerable with a select few trusted confidants who share your life.

Think about the greats in the world—the ballerina, moon walker, tennis star, racing driver etc. They will have lots of fans who see their GREAT performance and will eagerly listen to the winner's interview, waiting to glean a gem about what caused them to be so great. Many people listen to the winner to hear a technical advantage or a state of mind advantage or a particular strategy that caused this great outcome. However, more often than not, the great person first and foremost attributes the success to a few people for 'making this all possible'. Many of us listening to the great person's acknowledgement of these people make a number of assumptions:

1. The person can't accept the greatness and deflects it to the supporters—and we call it humility.
2. The supporting individuals were the reason for greatness. We say to ourselves 'if I had his wife, if only I had her coach, if I had his trainer, then I would be great, just like them'.
3. This great achievement is a result of a core team investing in the outcome and this person is the one who's committed the most effort—there's a group we don't even know about.

This last assumption, for a ME-centric society, is a hard one to accept. Intellectually we sort of 'get' it, yet many business owners and leaders don't know how to be it, do it or have it. What does it take to get over yourself and build a personal support team?

We've all had personal support in our life and I believe we have all achieved great things in our life. From the time we were born to now, as you are reading this book, you've had on occasion, in a particular time or area of your life, a select few people who relate to you without all the fanfare.

All people cry, argue, get angry, frustrated, obstinate, sad or grief stricken, are unmotivated, over-enthusiastic, crazy with crazy ideas, shallow and inconsiderate, make poor choices with money, are frugal or over-generous to their own detriment, and a whole heap of other stuff. We all do this when we are learning and growing. The greats, just like us, are human and are learning and growing too. And those last two words are the key, *they are learning and growing.*

We all became great walkers when we were toddlers because we 'learned how to walk' by falling over, bashing our heads on the kitchen table, walking into stationary objects, and dealing with uneven surfaces. We also had to contend with siblings pushing us and bumping into us, and parents and other people interrupting our walking learning by picking us up and carrying us. Some of us cried a lot, decided not to walk and demanded to be carried. Some of us had tantrums or were very cautious and moved slowly due to the massive bump we had the day before. Some of us didn't go near stairs and some of us had to deal with baby gates or barriers preventing us from learning at the rate we wanted to learn. Our parents, siblings and carers dealt with all the drama of it all. Yet, despite all that, we eventually learned how to walk. So when we arrived at a family or community event, people would watch us walk 'for the first time' and they would gush and praise us for walking so well and tell us how GREAT we were. Yet, there was a lot of effort and learning that caused that result.

We became great walkers because we exerted effort, and our parents, carers and family gave us feedback on what we were doing. They also encouraged and praised us for effective actions, gave us the reality of our efforts and obstacles, and let us be ourselves in the emotional management and mental and physical learning we had to go through, with as little judgement as possible because they knew we would get the hang of walking and do it successfully, eventually. They bore the brunt of our emotional and mental outbursts and breakdowns along the way. The people praising us and declaring us great, experienced none of that. How is this experience that we've all gone through in our life any different to anyone at any age becoming great at anything? It's not.

Now getting back to the scary word for many: TRUST.

If you are going to have greatness in any area of your life, you've got to be the toddler again and learn to walk in your new domain/area of life of greatness. You know it will be difficult, you're going to bump your head, have tantrums, do it wrong, do it right and you're going to have to build the muscles, neural pathways and mind/body/space co-ordination and way of being to make it work and be GREAT. Just like learning to walk, it's going to take some time, and you are going to need to find yourself some people to SUPPORT you. You are going to have to trust them to know the reality of where you currently are in your quest for greatness. They will know how much you have done or haven't done, and you must be prepared to take their advice, suggestions, warnings, strategies and encouragement to get the results you want. The question is … how badly do you want to be great or achieve greatness in the domain you are working on?

> *Watch your thoughts; they become words.*
> *Watch your words; they become actions.*
> *Watch your actions; they become habit.*
> *Watch your habits; they become character.*
> *Watch your character; it becomes your destiny.*
> ~ **Lao Tzu**

Chapter 3

Isolation doesn't work

In my work, I see many people who are isolated. I also see the devastating results of isolation. The following is an excerpt from a web page that deals with social isolation and its effects.

> **Isolation**—the experience of being separated from others—may result from being physically removed from others, as when a person lives in a remote area, or it can result from the perception of being removed from a community, such as when a person 'feels' socially or emotionally isolated from others. Social isolation is distinct from the experience of solitude, which is simply the state of being alone, usually by choice. Taking time to be alone can be a healthy, rejuvenating experience that allows us to reconnect with our own needs, goals, beliefs, values, and feelings. But when a person experiences too much solitude or feels socially isolated from others, he or she may develop feelings of loneliness, social anxiety, helplessness, or depression, among others.

Spending time alone is a good thing, and some people require more solitude than others. Introverts, for example, enjoy spending lots of time alone and can feel drained through social interaction, whereas extroverts prefer the company of others and are recharged through social interaction.

What is Social Isolation?

The absence of social relationships is typically considered unhealthy when people spend excessive time alone, particularly when they no longer benefit from time spent alone. Socially isolating oneself can mean staying home for days, not talking with friends or acquaintances, and generally avoiding contact with other people. Any form of contact, however limited, is likely to remain superficial and brief, while more meaningful, extended relationships are missing.

Social isolation may be indicated when a person's avoidance of social interaction:

- persists for an extended period of time
- is a result of depression, shame, or low self-worth
- is associated with abandonment fears or social anxiety
- proves detrimental to important social or professional relationships

Social isolation, in turn, can exacerbate a person's feelings of low self-worth, shame, loneliness, depression, and other mental health concerns. Thus, social isolation can be both a cause and symptom of other mental health issues. Isolation itself is not a diagnosis, but it can be a symptom of depression, social anxiety, or agoraphobia. Other conditions that impair social skills can lead to isolation, though not necessarily by choice.

What Is Emotional Isolation?

Emotional isolation can occur as a result of social isolation, or when a person lacks any close confidant or intimate partner. Even though relationships are necessary for our wellbeing, they can trigger negative feelings and thoughts, and emotional isolation can act as a defence mechanism to protect a person from emotional distress. When people are emotionally isolated, they keep their feelings completely to themselves, are unable to receive emotional support from others, feel 'shut down' or numb, and are reluctant or unwilling to communicate with others, except perhaps for the most superficial matters.

Emotional isolation can occur within an intimate relationship, particularly as a result of infidelity, abuse, or other trust issues. One or both partners may feel alone within the relationship, rather than supported and fulfilled. Identifying the source of the distress and working with a therapist to improve communication and rebuild trust can help couples re-establish their emotional bond.

From www.goodtherapy.org/therapy-for-isolation.html, used with permission.

Social isolation kills more people than obesity does and there is more and more research coming out showcasing this worldwide phenomenon. It's the silent problem that business leaders are NOT talking about. What makes matters worse is that, as we get more connected online, we are disconnecting from the personal and intimate relationships that people actually need to be Great. The illusion of being connected is just an illusion and we are all paying too high a price for it.

Loneliness is killing our leadership, businesses, families, communities and even our children, and nobody is really talking about it. Until I wrote this book and started researching the impact of social isolation, I never realised how lonely and disconnected we are becoming and that it is definitely affecting our mental, emotional, physical and spiritual health. When a person's health and wellbeing are down or critically low, who that person is being will have a massive impact on the world around them.

I was recently talking with a client (George) whom I hadn't seen in over 10 years. When I worked with him, his business was growing, his children were aged 10 and 13, and his marriage was strong. He hired me to take him and his business to the next level. We achieved that and more.

I arrived at the coffee shop where we had arranged to meet. I looked around, yet couldn't see him. So I went outside and there was a man whom I didn't recognise. George was a lot thinner, grey hair, and was hunched over checking his phone. He had low energy and when he saw me, he brightened a little bit and gave me a very long hug.

As we sat and caught up, he kept telling me all about the dramas and disasters that had happened to him over the past five years. His marriage had collapsed, he had been drinking heavily, and his business had gone broke. His children, now adults, no longer wanted anything to do with him. He had been broke most of the time and had part-time work as a tradesman. He now lives alone and hasn't managed to secure a flatmate to share the costs. He has had a few casual relationships that have not worked out well and he is currently seeing many professionals for his mental and emotional state. He is a former shadow of the courageous, fun-loving father and business man I worked with all those years ago and, to be honest, I felt like crying when I saw, heard and felt the state of his current life. It was heart-breaking.

Halfway through the conversation, when he had finished recounting his dramas, I interrupted with a question.

'So George, what's your vision for the future?'

He looked at me in shock and said, 'Jen, I don't know. I've been dealing with things day to day for so long.'

I acknowledged this and then spoke to him about the Greatness Principle®. I told him that for his life to work again and be GREAT, he needed to trust his Great8™ Investors. In that moment he leaned back and let out a huge sigh. He then looked at me very seriously and said, with despair, 'How can I trust anyone, when the people I loved and wanted to love me back rejected me and did things to me that broke my trust? My wife left me. My children rejected me. They are the ones that are supposed to care about me and want the best for me, and they don't.'

George, through a multitude of circumstances, had socially and emotionally isolated himself and now he didn't really trust anybody. He did have a few friends who suggested activities or gave him feedback on situations or events in his life, but George wasn't listening. He was so busy focussing on the past, and all the 'injustice' and wrongdoings, that he had become socially isolated, heavily medicated and deaf to the support that was coming at him ALL THE TIME.

The cost of isolation

The example of George, I'm sorry to say, is not an isolated case. Not everyone gets to George's extreme, and yet some go to the furthest extreme of suicide. The Australian Bureau of Statistics advises that only 47.5% of Australian businesses will survive the first five years from start-up. That leaves a massive 52.5% of businesses that will collapse.

As at 30th June, 2011, there were 2,045,335 actively trading small businesses in Australia.[1] If we then apply the 52.5% collapse rate to the actively trading small businesses, we expect 1,073,800 small businesses to break down within five years. Don't you think that is incredibly HIGH and alarming? I do.

Every leader in a collapsed business has a life that was affected by the business breakdown. Every business leader has a family (their own or siblings) that would have been affected by the breakdown of the business. Every one of these businesses had customers and suppliers that would have been affected.

Australia currently has a population of 23.5 million people. China has 1.3 billion, India 1.2 billion, United States 318 million, United

---

[1] Australian Bureau of Statistics ABS Cat. No 8165.0.

Kingdom 64 million. Imagine the number of small businesses and families that are attached to the businesses that are failing in those countries! This has got to stop! The cost is too high for all of us.

There has been no report or study anywhere to measure the real and true impact of business breakdown. It would be a major undertaking and I think it would be completely fascinating.

Breakdown and the reality check

Not every business breakdown will be the same. Some businesses will collapse and end because:

- The entrepreneur goes out into the world with a really dumb idea, convinces a lot of people to invest in it and then goes broke
- The business owner breaks the law or is corrupt
- The business owners and/or their staff make stupid, crazy decisions that kill the business.

However, in my experience, these people are in the minority. For all the people I've worked with, the breakdown has occurred when one of the leader's personal, health, business, family, sporting, or community domains had a problem occur in it, and because they kept that problem to themselves (sucked it up and got on with it) and didn't ask the right people for support. Their ability to lead, make decisions and adjust to the problem was ineffective. That weakness/vulnerability then caused them to cover up, disown, reject or ignore the problem, which, in turn, created more of a problem, and subsequent disconnection from the people who were supporting them in one or more areas of their life.

When we are not being honest with ourselves, when we hide, ignore, reject or cover up things, we instantly disconnect from reality. When we do that, we create stories, excuses, reasons, justifications and a context to hold 'it' in place. We then don't see things straight. We've all done it. I know I have. What is interesting is that, most of the time when 'stuff' happens in life, someone will say to you that you are being a jerk, you are not listening, you are making big mistakes or you're not being yourself, or even that something is up with you. This makes you 'snap out of it' and share your burden and challenge and open you up to get support, which brings you back to reality again and all the energy and focus you used 'covering up, managing or surviving' the problem can be used to deal with it.

What's interesting is that, in my experience, small business leaders typically DON'T share the challenges they are facing. Having been one myself for over 15 years, I know there's this 'thing' where many leaders want to prove they can do it by themselves. Maybe they have to prove it to an old boss, or to a family member, or to themselves that they can be someone they don't think they currently are. Maybe they have promised themselves that they 'can make this work' or can't talk about it due to a fear of failure ... there's a whole list of reasons. Whatever the reason, it makes it almost impossible for them to ASK FOR SUPPORT and TRUST that someone won't judge them, laugh at them or tell them that they are stupid for making such a mistake or not being able to handle a 'simple' situation.

Things people say when they are isolated

It's hard leading a business. It's even harder to be a pioneer in a new field or activity, service or creation. Our leaders and 'great' people need to feel safe to be able to share their humanity and their trials, struggles and successes as they move ahead. Some of the common things my own clients have said over the years when they were isolated in business are:

- I'm just too busy to talk right now.
- None of the staff really understand what's going on.
- I'm fine, really, now can we talk about business?
- I'm not tired; I was just up late/kids/client meetings.
- My wife and kids are having a break.
- I haven't talked to my family in years; that's not important.
- Why should I care about the community—I've got a business to run.
- Let's just stick to business; personal conversations aren't appropriate.

- I can't hire a book-keeper, my wife can do it.
- I'm not stupid, you know.
- It's only a small mistake, I can fix it.
- Don't tell me what to do, I've got it sorted.
- My husband is my rock. He's 'my everything'. I don't know where I'd be without him.
- Holidays! What are they?
- Yeah, my life's great. The business is profitable and it's working.
- It's all good. I wonder what the poor people are doing.
- No-one calls me or asks me to come to an event. I've got to initiate everything if I want it.
- Networking is for desperate people who want to sell you stuff.
- I'm not that interesting, really.
- I've got so many projects on at the moment, I'm flat out.

There is so much that could be said about isolation and its impact on our mental, emotional and physical health. I suspect I will co-write another book or two with experts who have seen and experienced social isolation's impact in other critical ways. My point with this chapter is to raise awareness about this silent problem. Our leaders are drowning in it, and many of them don't even know it; and those who do, aren't quite sure what to do about it and how to fix it.

What's the answer to isolation? There are probably many of them, depending on why a person is isolated. For the purposes of this book, though, I suggest the answer is in the application of the Greatness Principle® and the Greatness Wheel, which are explained in the next chapter.

> *People use drugs, legal and illegal, because their lives are intolerably painful or dull. They hate their work and find no rest in their leisure. They are estranged from their families and their neighbours. It should tell us something that in healthy societies drug use is celebrative, convivial, and occasional, whereas among us it is lonely, shameful, and addictive. We need drugs, apparently, because we have lost each other.*
> **~ Wendell Berry, *The Art of the Commonplace: The Agrarian Essays***

Chapter 4

The Greatness Principle®

Where did it come from?

Over the last 15 years, I've been a business coach, consultant and more recently a motivational speaker. Working directly coaching my clients, I've noticed patterns, common threads and nuances about this fascinating niche in which I have been immersed. The types of clients I have been working with fall into two main categories.

Entrepreneurs: single entrepreneurs, couples in business, and family businesses. Their ages ranged from 30 to 55 and they were mostly middle class Australians who were pursuing the dream of working hard, paying off the house and, if they were lucky, able to buy some investment properties as they went along and then eventually sell their business to realise their superannuation strategy. All of these people had goals and visions of using their business to create a better life for themselves, their staff and their customers. They were good people wanting to be better and make a difference in their chosen industry.

Chapter 4

The support they needed was diverse, however the main areas of need were: vision, personal awareness, character building and boundary setting, social isolation, and loneliness. They also needed support in how to sell, how to manage teams and how to keep life–work balance as the business grew.

Corporate Leaders: CEOs, department heads and special project leaders: men and women who were at the top of their game who wanted to go the next level in exceeding their targets and goals. Many of them wanted additional support in other areas of their life: money management, confidence, communication with their teams, and keeping life–work balance as their careers became even more demanding and intense.

My primary mission was to support my clients to achieve their goals and grow their businesses, their sales, and support them to create a life that worked. I definitely saw my work as business focussed. I've never really liked the term 'life coach', as I thought they were a bit on the light and fluffy side of coaching, and so I steered my style and clients into getting results (which they did in phenomenal ways), and keeping their feet on the ground as they achieved more, and felt even more elated with their accomplishments. Part of my role was grounding them, motivating them and keeping them accountable, creating strategies for them as well as celebrating achievements and milestones. I love my work and I love my clients, their courage, their commitment and their awesomeness. It really is a privilege and honour to be working with such committed, driven people who create great results for themselves, the people around them and the community in which they live and work.

However, in the early days of working with clients I started to notice that many of them who were getting great results were in fact dealing with a physical limitation such as ulcers, Crohn's Disease, mild heart attack, high blood pressure, grossly overweight, Type 2 diabetes, or some form of cancer that had been treated and was currently in remission. Initially I didn't think much of it and assumed that these things happen to people as we get older. Most of my clients were on average 40–55, so that 'seemed' about right. With that assumption, I adjusted my coaching, knowing that one in four would deal with a physical challenge, and so I supported them to use that to un-hook them from the business so they weren't so involved in the day-to-day activities. Michael Gerber's E-Myth® philosophy of 'work on the business and not in it' has been well and truly engrained in small businesses. So with that context, making sure the business was self-sufficient without them was a great idea because many business owners, CEOs and leaders would get sick and need time out. It wasn't until later that I realised that there was a possible reason WHY they were getting sick in the first place.

The next thing I noticed in about the 300th client was that a lot of leaders and business owners were in a state of depression. One coaching client, Kelvin, eventually plucked up the courage to say to me 'Jen, I can't do everything you've told me to do as I just can't do it. Life is so overwhelming and this business has been draining me for so long that I can only do so much. I've been to doctors and they have prescribed me anti-depressants and diagnosed me as clinically depressed.' He looked so ashamed. His wife stood there next to him as Kelvin went on and shared his reality. She was in tears, terrified that her husband was, at that time, so weak in his mind and overwhelmed by emotions. She looked worn down and physically exhausted from supporting him. She was drained too.

This revelation to me was incredible. These two lovely people, with good heads for business and the ability to deal easily with a wide range of people, were floundering and drowning in the responsibility of it. It didn't make sense. After Kelvin shared this with me, I went back over the list of clients I'd worked with so far and realised that a good third of them had exhibited the same responses to my coaching requests. The coaching had been hard for them and, upon reflection, I thought they may had been dealing with depression or a sense of isolation and were just not talking about it.

Chapter 4

So I called a few of them up to ask and most of them confirmed that YES, they had been diagnosed by their doctor and were on antidepressants and mood stabilisers to help them 'deal' with everything that was on their plate. They didn't want to tell me as they didn't think it was relevant (can you believe it?) and, more importantly, they were ashamed that they weren't coping with everything and hoped that the medicine would fix everything and they'd be able to go back to normal.

Now, as a trained and certified business coach, my job was to inspire clients to create visions and goals, motivate them to take action, hold them accountable and support them to navigate the world of business and leadership to be effective. I was great at that. My clients got great results, however I'd failed to notice that after coaching them for six to twelve months the coaching relationship had changed gears as I was now a trusted advisor to them (my client and their spouse/life partner), and I had started to support them with more personal goals and challenges as we had nailed the business issues.

This new relationship had changed. I had been 'adopted' by many of my clients as a close confidant. I knew all about them, their business, their relationships, and their family and how their world worked. I was in my early 30s. I was single and so I invested all of my time into my work, my business, friends, lifestyle and my family. I was a great Aunty Jen to my family's children and a solid supporter to my clients. I had the time and energy to give to my clients, and what was interesting was that they were taking it, even demanding it. The initial role of supporting them in their business endeavours was now focussed more on their personal issues.

They were attaching to me and, for many of them, claiming me as theirs. It was a bit flattering to begin with as I'd created so much value that they saw me as a vital part of their success. What I was beginning to get was that these people needed me more than I realised and that need was not healthy for me and it was draining me. I had 20–30 clients I was working with intensively every week as well as clients who were fortnightly on the phone or in person, plus speaking engagements all over the country every few weeks. I didn't have time to have a life of my own as my clients started pulling it from me and, of course, I let them.

I needed a strategy to support my clients to need me less because if I didn't do this, I was going to be over-worked, get sick and be overwhelmed by the demands of the people who were needing me and … Wait a minute! I was experiencing what my clients were going through! I wasn't physically in trouble yet, I was 36. Emotionally I was starting to feel like my client Kelvin and I'm sure I was starting to look like his exhausted wife. People were commenting on how tired I looked and that I needed to get more rest. Something was going on here and I was curious and desperate to change the demand and drain on my life from my clients, my business and how it was running.

Okay, I needed my clients to depend on me less. How could I do that? Some of them were so dependent on me. So I managed to take a few days off and reflected on what my clients were using me for. Many of them were working with me to grow their business and then after we'd done the work, they were telling me about all the life challenges they were facing. Oh my goodness, the things people told me about their lives were unbelievable. Many of them also wanted me to kick ideas and strategies around about what to do with their children (I was childless at that stage). They wanted advice and personal support in their relationships (I was a 36-year-old divorcee). A few of them wanted me to become their wife or at least their lover. Their words were 'I don't want to lose you, Jen. You mean so much to me, Jen, and you can't ever leave me/us'.

This powerful need to 'have me' and their sense of ownership of me freaked me out. It was 2007, and at that time I was living in the regional town of Bendigo, Victoria, Australia. The population of Bendigo and surrounds was about 100,000 people. I'd moved there the previous year because my mum had been diagnosed with a rare form of cancer—Multiple Myeloma. Mum's cancer threw our whole family into a spin and the outcome for me was that I chose to relocate

Chapter 4

from Sydney to be closer to Mum and Dad for as long as she had to live. Doctors estimated six months … well, she lived another six and a half years. My personal life in Bendigo for those six and a half years consisted of my parents, my work (and clients), and my sister and brothers who'd come to visit more often as mum was sick. I had gained three close girlfriends in Bendigo and I remained connected to my best friends who were living in Perth, Brisbane and Moss Vale, NSW. I didn't have a long-term boyfriend or partner, so I focussed on my mum, work, family and friends.

So, back to figuring out how to deal with my clients' need of me. I was out in the back yard one day, visiting my Dad. His name is Bob. Mum (Cath) was asleep inside the house. Bob was watering his veggies. The back garden was lush and vibrant. Bob was 64 and had retired almost a year before to take care of Cath. So with that life change, he invested in new pursuits and growing vegetables, roses, garlic, snow pea flowers and stone fruit was one of his hobbies and pure joy. I came down the back and sat on a ledge and told Bob about how my clients

Dad's garden

were wanting more and more from me personally and that it didn't feel right. I shared with him that I was concerned that I might lose my clients if I pulled back from them or rejected their requests, and that wouldn't be good for business, yet their need/almost demand for me wasn't good for me or the business either. He listened. Bob's great at that. After a while he said:

'You are being too much for them. They don't have balance. You don't have balance. You need to figure out where your boundary is for your coach role and support them find other people or activities to balance them out. Your mother is very sick and when she is asleep I use the garden to keep balance.'

Bob actually did a lot of things to keep balanced. He listened to the world on his radio. At night and very early in the morning, he would listen to the news from all over the world. He loved it. Bob also had a couple of men friends whom he would visit every week or two and discuss religion, politics and life with. Bob also was a part of the University of the Third Age, a community for retired and senior people who want further education in many areas of life. Bob also founded the Bendigo Cancer Support Group with Cath.

Bob's sweet peas

Bob was doing one of the hardest jobs in life—full time care for your dying spouse. We were clear, she was going to die from this disease, it was just a matter of when. It was a hard job for Bob as Cath had lots of chemo, special drugs, operations, side effects and massive pain

Chapter 4

management challenges. Her mood swings were big, her mental capacity ebbed and flowed due to the drugs she was taking and her physical strength fluctuated from strong to weak to frail and then strong again. She was ever changing as her cancer was complicated and her reactions to treatment were changing too.

Cath nearly died three times and Bob remained her Anchor (her rock) the whole time. To keep Cath alive and support her, Bob was in balance with great support from his children, friends, the support group, his garden, Cath herself and all sorts of people he listened to all over the world on his radio. Bob's Vision was to love his wife with all of his life. Bob's Personal Awareness was well developed. He adjusted his behaviour and thinking to deal with an unpredictable sick person whom he loved more than anything and Bob's character … he's a man of his word, honours a handshake deal, and treats all people with love, respect and dignity. His character was then, and still is, solid and inspiring. And his personal support network was so full and strong that it caused Bob to do his job magnificently, caring for

Family - Kate, me, Peter, Mum, Dad, Brad

Cath until her very last breath in October 2010. Cath and Bob were married for 42 years and 22 days!

So when Bob said to me in the back garden, 'they don't have balance and neither do you, Jen', he knew what he was talking about. Then, in true Bob fashion, he left me to figure out how to solve the puzzle, something I was very keen to do. So I went back to my office and reflected on the 100 clients who had, in the past, needed me the most. I looked at where the connection with me was the strongest and the 'dependency' was the most obvious. I then compared them to the top 100 clients who didn't depend on me or have an attachment. These clients used my service, skills and abilities, however many of them didn't 'need' me for everything. They took my perspective, point of view and ideas and then talked it through with other people in their life until they came up with a solution. These clients were balanced and what was interesting was that most of the business owners/leaders had been married or been in a long-term relationship for over 15 years. They weren't divorced and could tell me the stories of

Mum and Dad

when they nearly did get divorced! They had solid relationships with their teenage or adult children. They still talked to their parents (if still alive) and siblings and they had a solid support network. Most of the coaching I did with these people was around vision, sales strategy and accountability. Their character was strong and their personal awareness was high.

On the flip side, the more dependant/needy clients didn't have a clear vision, they weren't as personally aware of who they were and the impact they had on others, and their character was weak in many areas. They lacked discipline and focus. The biggest realisation was that they had a maximum of only three people (mostly it was two) in their entire world that they confided in and talked deeply with. These 2–3 people were their spouse/partner, their accountant and me. With everyone else they didn't share anything personal. They didn't trust anyone else to confide in. They were what I call a Lone Wolf.

> Wikipedia Definition: Lone Wolf
>
> As an animal, a lone wolf is a wolf that lives independently rather than with others as a member of a pack. In the animal kingdom, lone wolves are typically older wolves driven from the pack, perhaps by the breeding male, or young adults in search of new territory. Many young wolves between the ages of one and four years leave their family to search for a pack of their own (this has the effect of preventing inbreeding), as in typical wolf packs there is only one breeding pair. Some wolves will simply remain lone wolves; as such, these lone wolves may be stronger, more aggressive and far more dangerous than the average wolf that is a member of a pack. However, lone wolves have difficulty hunting, as wolves' favorite prey, large ungulates, are nearly impossible for a single wolf to bring down alone. Instead, lone wolves will generally hunt smaller animals and scavenge carrion.
>
> As a person, a lone wolf is an individual who prefers solitude, is introverted, or who works alone.

In literature, lone wolves are aloof and emotionally unable or unwilling to directly interact with other characters in the story. A stereotypical lone wolf will be dark or serious in personality; they are often taciturn, and will distinguish themselves through their reserved nature.

A similar concept is the lone wolf of a particular group, who spends enough time with a group to be considered a member but not enough time to be very close to the other members. Such people tend to not take part in the group activities or 'get-togethers'.

In military or security groups, such lone wolves frequently act on their own accord, insist on working alone, refuse to work with most of if not all members of the group and/or go against the plans of missions/operations and attempt to complete said task alone.

http://en.wikipedia.org/wiki/Lone_wolf_%28trait%29, reproduced here under Creative Commons Attribution 2.5 Generic License (CC BY 2.5)

Just as the definition above sums up lone wolves in four different contexts, the business Lone Wolf leaders that I've been coaching don't have a group for support either. For a variety of reasons, they are on their own and they are actually struggling personally to deal with it. They've latched onto a spouse or partner (again for a variety of reasons) and that partner now bears the burden of supporting their Lone Wolf. If the business or the job goes okay, the partner can cope. If it doesn't go well, they both suffer and their need for support grows. Anyone who comes into their inner world, like I do as a business coach, will be pounced upon and latched onto as the Lone Wolf has miraculously let their guard down, opened themself up and therefore want to protect their vulnerability and at the same time get support to stop the downward spiral of their career, their business, their money, the demise or breakdown of their marriage or their own personal health and wellbeing.

This whole phenomenon, we all know. We see it all the time. Yet we don't see it. Having been through it myself in a variety of forms in my life, I believe we have been conditioned to think that we need to search within ourselves to find the answers and that we need to work on ourselves. Over the last 20–30 years, personal development programs have drummed into us that we need to be better. We need to work on ourselves so we can be more powerful, more effective and more productive. The pressure to be better, earn more, get the things 'we deserve' and compete with everyone else because they want the same thing is totally exhausting and has a shallowness about it.

We've also created and accepted the reality that being a Lone Wolf is essential and critical to be successful as a leader and a business owner. As the Wikipedia definition states, 'lone wolves have difficulty hunting, as wolves' favourite prey … are nearly impossible for a single wolf to bring down alone. Instead, lone wolves will generally hunt smaller animals and scavenge carrion'. This is what happens in business. Many Lone Wolf leaders with great potential and ability don't have the resources or support network to take top leadership positions or bigger deals and opportunities because they are busy chasing smaller deals to survive week to week or month to month and taking on any kind of work to make ends meet. The lone wolves in business are in the constant state of trying to survive in an environment that could actually provide bountiful opportunity and long-term deals—if only they would start asking for and receiving support from each other.

It's CRAZY!

Yet it's happening every day in many small businesses and in leaders' lives and families all over the world! So I started asking even more questions and looking even harder. What support do we need to be great?

Creating the Greatness Wheel

Over time I started to put the pieces of the puzzle together. Please know that I didn't go searching for models, theories and other definitions. I didn't even look. I was on a personal mission wanting to answer the question of how do I support my clients so they can be in balance. I began studying my own data, extensive client base and personal experience. I was processing physical information, business results and achievements, perceived emotional states of clients, their spouses, their families and their staff, the mental capacity and ability to thrive during challenging times as well as a perceived sense of self, calm and awareness. Also, many of my clients believe in a higher power. They are from a variety of denominations yet they all have a relationship with God or the Universe. So I was also assessing and reviewing their perceptions of how strong their connection with God was or how well everything kept 'flowing in their universe'.

Even though I have a science degree from the University of New South Wales, Sydney, Australia, none of this 'research' or inquiry was done in a scientific way. It was pieced together over five years with me coaching people and thinking, reflecting, asking questions, getting answers, testing a new theory/model angle and then seeing how it worked with clients and if it resonated with them. If it did connect with them, I'd then look to see if it caused them to take action and change their circumstances and results. My focus was not to explain what was going on. My mission was to find out how to fix it.

So, in all of the hundreds of clients I reviewed and spoke with, there were commonalities between the support people who were active in their lives, the results they were getting and the level of balance they experienced. It boiled down to this: *for leaders to have balance, they need eight active relationship roles with people they feel they can trust and be vulnerable with.*

Chapter 4

The Greatness Wheel: Your Great8™

There are eight pieces of the wheel. Each represents an investor relationship. I call them our Greatness Investors—your Great8™. Each of these people takes on a role in your wheel and they consciously choose to invest in YOU.

These people all understand your vision, they are as personally aware or even more personally aware of themselves as you and they have the character, values and virtues that your vision lives in. You may not have the character habits, beliefs, behaviours, strategies, non-judgement, wisdom, mental approach or 100% enthusiasm on how to achieve your vision—yet—however, collectively the Great8™ people have all of it and more to share with you and support you in your development.

The Great8™ are an extension of your vision and the best tool for you to achieve it. When you are striving to create or achieve something great, it's not always easy and, if it is, you are almost always faced with distractions, interruptions, diversions, barriers and reasons to stop. In all of my work with hundreds of clients, I realised that the Great8™ are a leader's insurance policy and stabilising factor to ensure the leader doesn't get off track, and bounces and bumps back, rather than smashing, breaking and stopping.

The Great8™ life ring analogy

Imagine jumping off a big ship in the middle of the ocean. You are thrown a life ring. You get into the middle of it. It holds you up, keeps you floating. It gives you the ability to see above the waterline. You can rest in/on it when you get tired. It is true support and by its very nature, it allows you to be in control. You are the one who must paddle or swim to move forward. You make the choices as to how fast or slow you are going to move and in which direction. The life ring is there 100% for as long as you need it, whether you decide to swim back to the ship, or go in the other direction for another ship or swim to dry land/your treasure island!

In many cases, people jump out of corporate life or a large company and start their own business. They were typically successful in the corporate world, however they ended up frustrated by the lack of speed, responsiveness or integrity of the large company and, having created a better vision for themselves or the customers they served (or both), the employees jump off and go out into the sea of small business WITHOUT a life ring. They have so much passion, energy and determination that they start swimming away from the big ship and even attract others who've recently jumped off their 'ship' to join them. After a while (6, 12 or 18 months) of swimming hard, the leaders of the small businesses get tired. They can't see above the waterline, they've got a lot of people depending on them, choices and decisions need to be made and the leaders can't see any other leader in sight to share with or learn from and, if they do, the other leader is just as exhausted and feeling responsible for the activity created.

Chapter 4

The leaders then turn to the people in the water swimming with them who started with them early on. They assume the other swimmers have the same vision and drive to be there. They don't, they are followers, not leaders. They have little to contribute or support the leaders with and the leaders again are feeling unsupported and even more tired.

Pretty soon another ship comes by and the leaders have options: to get out of the water and get back on the ship to rest, recover and regain composure and strength, or to accept a life ring that's thrown over to them. 'Do you need any help, mate?' the people on the ship call out to the leaders who have their heads down swimming as hard as they can. 'No, thanks, I'm good', reply the leaders or, sometimes, the leaders are so busy swimming, they don't or can't hear the offers of support. Life rings may be thrown at them, but they don't even see them and swim past.

Does this sound like you or someone you know? Are you someone who has offered support, thrown someone a life ring and to your surprise and disappointment, that someone didn't see it, take it or accept it? What became of that person? Did they go on to achieve greatness or are they doing averagely or okay? In your opinion, could their results have been even greater if they had accepted support, listened to advice and generally been supported?

I believe the time has come for us all to stop being so independent, so isolated and such lone wolves. It's not working and it's actually killing us, breaking down key relationships and affecting our children in a profound way.

We are growing and learning in all areas ALL THE TIME. Learning and growing isn't easy and, just like little kids, we are going to have mixed feelings, ideas and opinions about it, and that is normal. Similarly, it's time for us to recognise that there are other people who genuinely do want the best for us, who want to contribute to us and have something valuable to give. We must allow others to contribute by trusting and being vulnerable with them. And finally we must stop discarding people and relationships for simple reasons because they might say something we don't like, disagree with us, not stay in contact enough, challenge us or point out the reality of our situation and circumstances.

Note: If you are in a relationship with someone who is harmful to your physical, mental or emotional health, then of course seek professional support and advice immediately.

Chapter 4

*No-one ever becomes great and stays
great all by themselves.*
~ Jen Harwood

Chapter 5

The Greatness Investor roles

Consider yourself, for this moment, at the centre of the universe. When you are in the centre, you can see all around you, a full 360 degrees of all the possibilities and potential before you. However, the challenge of being in the centre is that you will always have blind spots no matter which direction you turn. You will always be dealing with the problem of … you don't know what you don't know!

Lone wolves know this and adapt, change and innovate to survive the conditions to minimise vulnerability and weakness. The down side of this is that a majority of their thinking is focussed on survival and protection and just getting through the day. There is no time for the bigger picture and even thinking or acting to change the harsh circumstances they face.

The successful and thriving businesses and leaders I've worked with recognised it was essential to have perspective, reflection and a safe place to share intimate details and experiences (both good and bad) in order to be able to learn, grow and develop quickly. By working with their trusted confidants, they had the ability to RESPOND to their environment rather than just REACTING.

The Greatness Principle® is based on creating eight trusted, confidant relationships in your business/work and life. These relationships form your support team. They are invested in you and committed to your success. They form your Greatness Wheel and are called your Great8™. They are used as a reflection and mirror to support you to understand who you are, where you should focus your attention, what's important, what you should stop doing, and cause you to grow, expand and nurture your ideas and celebrate your magnificence.

The eight Investor roles cover all aspects of being in Spirit, Emotion, Body and Mind. They are:

Enthusiast: supports your optimism, energy and possibility
Sage: supports your authenticity, wisdom and freedom
Motivator: supports your commitment, action and accountability
Bystander: supports your interest, information and perspective
Anchor: supports your belief, confidence and pride
Grounder: supports your realism, scepticism and practicality
Catalyst: supports your incitement, challenge and growth
Scholar: supports your ideas, intellect and consequences

Each Investor role is explained below, to help you find yours and be one to others.

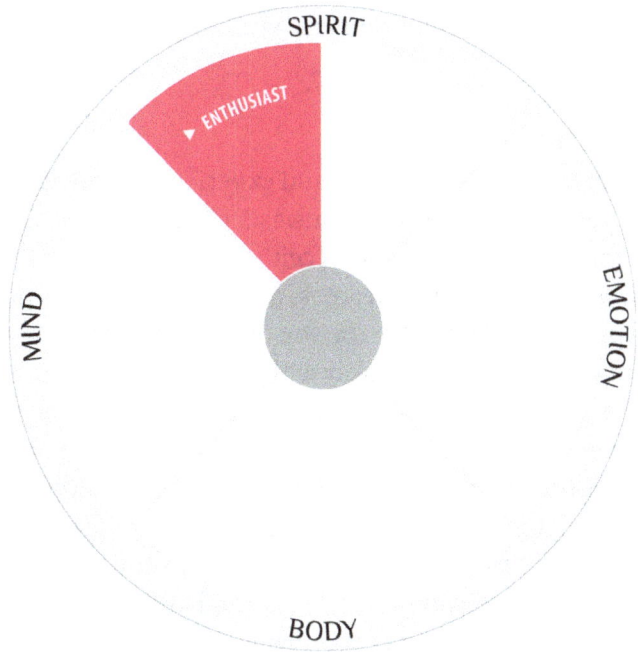

Enthusiast: optimism, energy, possibility

i. Eternally OPTIMISTIC is how the Enthusiast sees you. No matter what you do, how you screw something up or if you fail, the Enthusiast brushes that aside and sees and remembers all the great things about you and your life. How awesome is that? They are a walking, cheering, excited FAN of YOU all the time.

ii. You get ENERGY from this person. When you see them they are excited, thrilled, engaged and energised by YOU and want to know what great things are going on for you now. Even if you are having a bad day, they have the ability to draw out greatness and give you energy to try again, keep going or go higher!!!

iii. In their mind, the POSSIBILITY for you and your life/career/business is endless and they have an unwavering belief about you that you will achieve your dreams/goals. They are also a little 'in awe of you', and that's fantastic. The Enthusiast is inspired by you and sometimes will hang off your every word. Their optimism and energy enable you to also dream more, lift higher and believe in new possibilities for you and your life.

How to relate to the Enthusiast
- They will re-tell your stories and experiences to others, so make sure you tell the truth. Enthusiasts are devastated if they find out you are full of lies and deceit.
- They will tap into your greatness and use it in their own life. They will pretend in their life to be you or do what you do to give them courage and strength. Be okay with this. Greatness is an unlimited resource. When others emulate you, use a strategy you've shared, or generally copy you, be okay with it. You are a light of hope and a leader into greatness. Let them follow in your footsteps.
- Do not tell them how much of a loser, phoney or fake you are with them. We all feel we are these things from time to time. Let the Enthusiast tell you how great you are and just take it on board. Use their energy to snap out of your own self-pity and self-destruction.
- This is the person to celebrate with. All of your other Investors are too, of course, however this Investor LOVES celebration. When you share the smallest win/achievement, tell them. They will love it and it will build momentum.
- Remember, in some area of their life, you are their HERO. They love who you are and where you are going. Don't ever kill that for them.

How to be the Enthusiast
- You are completely inspired by your subject in some aspect of their life. It may be their attitude, their results or just who they are being in this world that just 'does it for you'!
- Listen to them BIG! See them as the future person they want to be and talk to them as that. Don't accept their smallness, complaints, should haves, could haves, would haves. You are not interested in their negative thoughts of themselves or their life. Remind them of their greatness.

- Share their own stories back to them of success, funny things they did or said. Share other stories that are inspiring and funny to connect your subject to their possibility.
- Use your subject's greatness. Yes, that's right, when you get stuck in your life, ask yourself, how would (insert your subject's name) handle this? You will be amazed at what comes to mind and you can temporarily step into your subject's greatness and expand your life. Share those results with your subject.

Investor warning

Remember, your subject is a HUMAN BEING, not GOD. All people will make mistakes, screw up and make bad choices. That's the time to be with your subject, to remind them how great they are. However, some people, when their Greatness Wheel isn't full, may experience lots of bad things and start to become a lot more negative and destructive.

Remember, your strengths of optimism, energy and possibility can be your greatest weaknesses when your subject is in breakdown. Your lightness and bounce in their life may not be appreciated as they may have too much negativity and disconnect you from their life. On the flip side, your subject might get very destructive and start using you as a crutch as they get rid of all their other Investors and rely on you telling them they are great when clearly at the time they are not being great at all. They may be violent, abusive, controlling or dominating. If this is the case, you need to still see them as a great person who is behaving badly and take immediate action. Take a step back, see the current reality and protect yourself from any physical, mental or emotional drain or danger.

Also, it's advisable that you make sure you know who some of your subject's other Investors are so you can ask them to support your subject when they are in breakdown. The best Investors for this are usually the Anchor, the Grounder and the Motivator, as they talk it straight, don't take excuses and can usually snap your subject out of their destructive thinking and actions.

Chapter 5

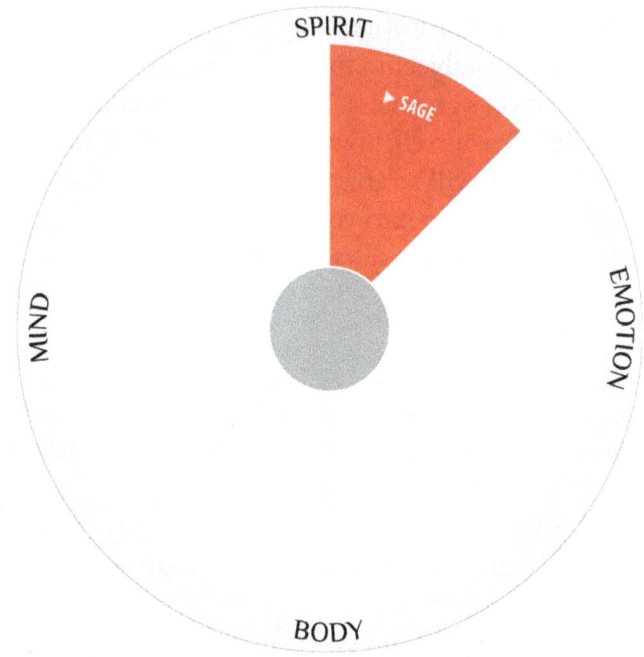

Sage: authenticity, wisdom, freedom

i. They know the real YOU without any of the masks or bravado that you may put out there as Superman or Wonder Woman! In many cases, these people have known you for a long time, such as a family member or someone you've known since you were a child. They have seen you grow older and also seen/experienced the patterns in your life. This investor keeps you on track for you to be AUTHENTIC.

ii. The Sage, as the name suggests, has WISDOM for you. The Sage does not need to be an 'old' person to fill this role. The wisdom they provide is advice and support with respect to knowing you better than most people. They comment on what's best for you, given your history and personality.

iii. When you are with this person you are totally FREE to be yourself—however that is. Of all the people in your life, they have seen the best and worst of you, your actions and behaviour. They accept you for who you are and this creates a space for you to let go and just BE. When you do this, inspiration and great ideas can flow as there is no effort by either of you to DO anything. It is a spiritual, heartfelt connection between you both of acceptance and love.

How to relate to the Sage
- They are someone you completely trust with every piece of information about you and your life. They will keep it confidential. Tell them everything.
- Tell them the truth, even if you don't want to. This Investor knows when you are lying, so don't insult them with fabrications or omit information.
- Ask them for their perspective and thoughts as they know you best: their answers will be through their knowledge of you.
- Really listen to them and ACCEPT their advice. Of all of your investors, this one really knows you well and has history about you that's worth relying on.
- Tell them you love them. Out of all your Investors, this one has been with you through everything in your life. They deeply love you in their life and when you tell them, they may brush it off, however they do like to hear it.
- Also know that the Sage is the guardian of your Greatness. As they usually have the longest relationship with you, they are keeping watch and monitoring who is in your life and Greatness Wheel. They naturally pay attention to who you are keeping company with and if they tell you that a person you're hanging around with probably isn't good for you … pay attention. Most of the time, they will be right and you need to do something about that sooner rather than later.

How to be the Sage
- In a way, you're the record keeper of your subject's life. You're the friend at parties who can tell the most stories about your subject as you've been with them the longest.

- Don't feel pressure with this role to always be there for them every day in every way. That's not your job.
- Remember your timing and intuition about your subject is always spot on in a spooky kind of way. Embrace that and always share your thoughts, ideas and advice.
- Know that the best thing you can do for your subject is to be available and someone who can listen to them in good and bad times.
- Do not judge them or try to fix them. Just point out options and choices and let them freely choose. The more you can do this, the more they will trust you and the more you will learn through their choices and experiences, building your own wisdom and Sageness!
- The greatest gift you give is having your subject 'being known' on a deep level.

Investor warning

There will be times when your subject isn't always going to be close to you. You may disagree, get upset or you may have things happen in your life that consume your attention and energy. There may be weeks, months or a few years that you might not be in close communication. Be okay with that. Try to stay connected with a phone call, email or visit as often as you can. Being close or not doesn't diminish your great contribution and power to your subject's Greatness. You're a witness to their entire life and this is a very valuable point of view and asset for them.

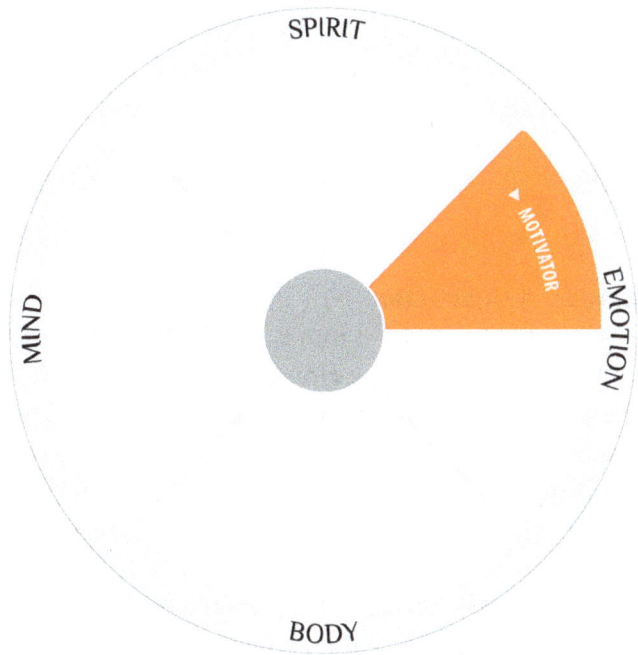

Motivator: commitment, action, accountability

i. Talk is good, COMMITMENT gets results. The Motivator has the ability to cut through all your small talk, excuses, distractions, issues, challenges and reasons and get to the heart of your dreams/results and take it on themselves as if the dream/result you have is their own. They will own it 100% and will get you to commit to it even more than you did when you first shared it with them. This level of commitment puts your dream/goal into reality and on track for success.

ii. ACTION is essential. The Motivator will get you out of your comfort zone. They'll ask you to do things you won't feel ready to do. Do them anyway. You will expand as a person and it might not feel good doing this. Do it anyway. They will also offer you opportunities that can fast track your results. You'll have to give something up and change to accept the opportunity. Just give it up/change and do it anyway.

iii. ACCOUNTABILITY is their focus and at times it will be your dread. Everyone else in your life may skirt over your excuses and reasons: the Motivator won't. They can scare you as you know you can't hide or pretend with them and why would you want to? They champion your dream and are prepared to kick your stagnancy to make it happen for you.

How to relate to the Motivator
- The Motivator has bought into your vision/dream and wants it more for you than you do. How can that be possible? They are not as emotionally attached to the outcome as you. They can see the benefits to you and others clearly and sincerely want you to stop talking and wishing about what you want and just do it.
- Use their passion and energy to drive you forward even when you don't have the energy or passion yourself.
- Know that when they scare you, when you feel uncomfortable, when you feel like not doing something they have requested, you are moving closer to the results you want.
- Update them with your activity—the good, bad and the ugly.
- Tell them everything. They need to know what's really going on for you to be able to help you deal with obstacles and challenges.
- Remember, the Motivator's vision of your goal is only as good as you communicate it. You have the core vision of your dream/goal, so protect, nurture and share it with them.

How to be the Motivator
- You must fully own their dream/goal.
- Do NOT for any reason get involved in their dream/goal. Remain emotionally detached and independent.
- Don't take any nonsense such as excuses, reasons or distractions.
- Coaching and communication training can really deliver outstanding results for your subject.
- Listen for your subject's commitment and encourage them to take action.

- Keep them moving small steps forward, even if they are experiencing challenging times.
- Tough love is required. Your role is not to be liked: it is to be respected. Of all the people on the Greatness Wheel, you demand respect and results.
- Allow your subject to make choices and decisions that you might not agree with. Don't make them wrong, as their vision/goal is in their head and you only have an interpretation of what it really is.

Investor warning

As you have bought into their dream and vision, when your subject starts to get results it may be very tempting to get physically or emotionally involved and jump into their picture. My advice is DON'T. If you do, you will immediately lose your effectiveness as you are no longer unbiased, independent and as tough with your requests as you are now in the picture, not outside looking objectively at it. If the role of Motivator is not replaced with someone else, your subject's Greatness will weaken and there is a potential for them to slacken off and make you the person responsible and accountable for their dream/goal. In some cases I've worked with, the subject has delegated complete responsibility over to the involved Motivator or, on the flip side, the Motivator has eagerly taken over and the subject became angry, resentful, destructive and miserable as the actions and activities being taken weren't really making their dream/goal come true: they were making the Motivator's interpretation of it come true. So if you jump into the picture, change roles to Enthusiast and find them a new Motivator quick smart.

Chapter 5

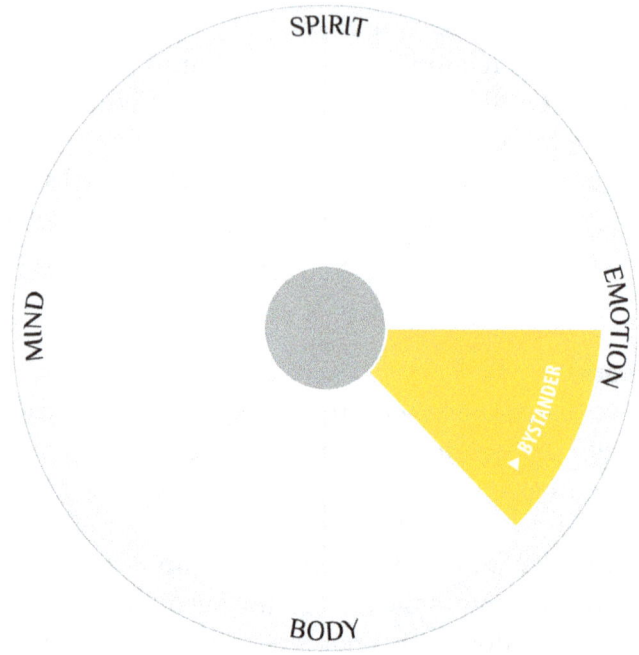

Bystander: interest, information, perspective

i. The Bystander is outside of your normal field of activity or focus. You have an affinity or shared values with them and for some reason, they find YOU very INTERESTING. They genuinely are curious about how you are, what you are doing and how you are doing it. In conversations, they remember details you have told them (and then forgotten because you deem them trivial) and ask you about them the next time you catch up some weeks/months/years later.

ii. INFORMATION is the currency of this relationship. You share with them the happenings and facts of situations and your world. They in turn will share information with you about situations and happenings in their world. As you share, you learn more about yourself. As they ask questions and explore further into the detail, the more you hear yourself talk about how you feel about what's happening in your life/business/career. This is good.

Also, your Bystander learns with you as your awareness expands and develops.

iii. PERSPECTIVE is the greatest gift that the Bystander relationship gives both of you. There are many lessons in life and it's a lot easier to learn though others' actions, results, mistakes and failures. As they share what's going on for them and vice versa, you both pick up strategies, insight and wisdom in realms of life not in your usual focus. This support 'rounds you out' into a more full, educated and interesting person. All too often we just focus on what is important to us and shut out the rest of the world. It is okay to get your head down and focus, however, life wants you IN it, not just in a tiny part of it. Your Bystander lets you learn through them, and they do the same through you.

How to relate to the Bystander
- Have lots of Bystanders for areas of life you are interested in and don't have time to dwell in. An occasional catch up with each of them will energise, inspire and educate you.
- It's YOUR job to organise to catch up with them. Don't be the one saying, 'they haven't called or made contact in ages and it's not my fault!!!' Stop that and re-establish the connection immediately. It's good for both of you.
- Remember that your Bystander is always innocent. Their agenda is to hang out with you because you are fun and safe to be with. Listen to them, share with them.
- Remember this Investor is 'not attached' to your life or outcomes. They will sometimes say things you won't like or will disagree with, be okay with this, as they are sharing with you a perspective you wouldn't normally consider.
- Consider having Bystander Investors who are in the areas and realms of life you want to be in in the future, and start spending time with them.

Chapter 5

How to be the Bystander
- Be yourself and share your life. You trust your subject completely as you've been friends for enough time to trust them with details.
- Do not judge your subject. When you meet with them it's like turning on the TV or going to a movie. For a couple of hours you are going to immerse yourself in another world. There will be stories, situations, drama, laughter and the full human experience. It's their life and they are sharing it with you. Let them.
- Listen to your subject from the place of learning and interest. 'Listening for the Gold or Wisdom' in what they are saying will enable you to do this at a deeper level.
- Remember, you don't have to fix anything, do anything or get involved. Actually, it's better for everyone if you don't.
- If you do find yourself getting involved in your subject's life, recognise that your Great8™ Investor role has changed and it is best that you work out which new role you are being and adapt to the expectations and boundaries of that relationship.

Investor warning
For people who are having success in their life, your role further expands and strengthens their ability and results by giving them a richness of awareness and insight into a bigger picture. However, for people who are contracting and reducing their Greatness, your role is one that is easily forgotten, and people don't have time to be with you. This is par for the course for this role: there is a casualness to it that can be deemed unimportant and not relevant. Don't be offended that your subject has been out of contact. If they are out of communication with you, they are probably experiencing breakdown. If you wait for them to re-engage, you could be waiting a really long time. So don't wait for them to contact you. Do it yourself. That could be a phone call, catch up, skype call, or go to a movie … anything that has you back in communication. It's actually good for you too.

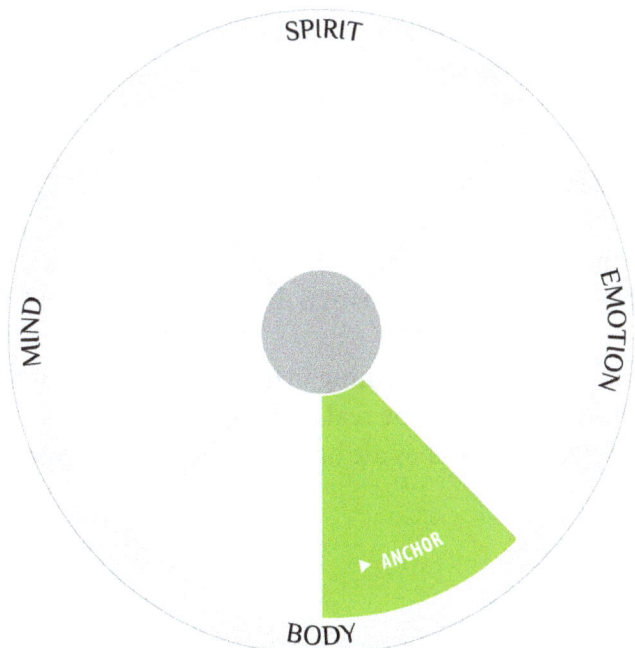

Anchor: belief, confidence, pride

i. They have unwavering BELIEF about you. They see you as your full potential and relate to you as that potential. They don't listen to the little stories about how unworthy you think you are, how you're not capable and how 'it' cannot be done. These people believe in your capability and talk in end results, knowing you'll figure it out as you go.

ii. They ooze CONFIDENCE in your ability. Sometimes that may scare you, as they believe it more than you do—that's okay, that's why they are in your life. Also, this is the person to tell your great big ideas and plans to. They will not shoot you down. They won't over-exaggerate them with you either. They will support you to discover yourself to be able to realise your dreams.

iii. Of all the Investors, this one is the most PROUD of you. Your greatness and success in life affects this Investor the most. I have found that people who are in the most serious of breakdowns get out of it if they are connected to this investor and are talking to them regularly—daily or weekly—until the drama is less and the balance is more.

How to relate to the Anchor
- Trust their belief in you—even when you don't believe in yourself.
- Use their confidence as a booster.
- Tell them about your plans and dreams: let them build on it with you.
- When you achieve something in life, tell, show and involve them.
- Tell them the truth—be real and honest.
- Respect them: who they are being for you is an extremely valuable gift.

How to be the Anchor
- Your love and commitment for the person you are anchoring is deep and unquestionable.
- Talk straight and make the conversation about them.
- Tell them you are proud of them when they get a result in any area of life.
- When they tell you their plans and dreams, encourage them.
- Share your own or others' stories about greatness, triumph, victory and success.
- Tell them and show them they CAN be, do and have anything, and that you believe that with all your heart.
- You must hold your character strong and be solid and reliable for your subject. If your world collapses, it will have a big impact on the people you anchor. If your world does collapse or change, don't be a martyr, tell your subject straight away and have them bring someone else into their Great8™ quickly. Know that you need support too, so ask your subject for assistance if that is appropriate.

Investor warning

This role is an important one. You need to make sure that you have your Greatness Wheel complete or near complete, as being the Anchor for someone who is experiencing hard times, breakdown, bankruptcy and other low times in their life is extremely draining and time consuming. Be aware that being an Anchor for someone could take time away from you developing and nurturing your own Great8™ network. You must make sure that you keep perspective and balance in your own life. You can do this by gently bringing in other Investors into your subject's wheel. The more people who can invest time, energy, love, thoughts, ideas and conversation into their life, the easier the load is for all, especially you, and everyone can keep moving forward. Be mindful that you only anchor one person at a time who is experiencing major breakdown unless you are a trained professional!

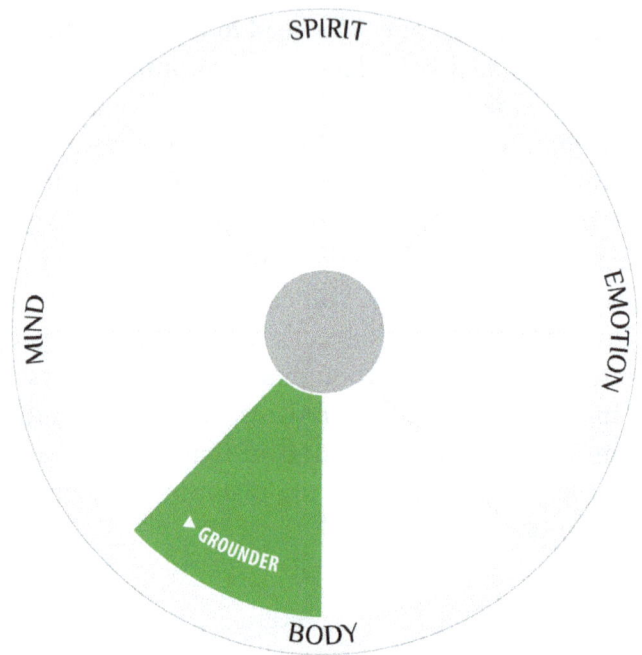

Grounder: realist, sceptic, practical

i. They are people grounded in REALITY. When you share what you are up to or plan to do, they go into automatic pilot and think of all the facts and details and start to calculate how it's all going to work and how you and others might be affected. They also say what needs to be said regardless of whether you will like them or accept them. It's their duty to declare reality.

ii. They are also SCEPTICAL of your ideas, plans or actions. This might be in their general personal nature or you've created them to be sceptical of you based on your past broken promises, failed grand plans and half-baked ideas that have fallen through. Yes, many of us create our own sceptics and that's a very good thing. Sceptics remind us of our limitations and mistakes, not because they are cruel or mean. They do this because they don't want you or others to get hurt or fail again!

iii. They are also PRACTICAL people who will want to give you strategies, advice, names of people to contact who will support you, and are excellent people who follow through and get things done. They are more focussed on the DOING and results than anything else.

How to relate to the Grounder
- They like to organise and get into the facts and details. My advice to you is: let them.
- Remember, pointing out reality is what they naturally do. They are not wrong for doing it and they are not judging you. They are sharing the reality of the current circumstances you are in and/or potential choices you are about to make.
- Remember, you need this perspective in your life, even if you don't want it or don't like it.
- Thank them for their contribution, acknowledge they are making a difference to you.
- Tell them when their advice and point of view has been right. Let them gloat. They like to be right AND they will be more likely to be your Grounder for bigger, more important issues.

How to be the Grounder
- This is a very important role for your subject. You are the devil's advocate and cynic.
- Embrace this role, as it is critical for your subject's success.
- Make them think about what they are doing, and do not judge them. They can't see what you see. They don't know what you know, so it could be hard for them to 'get it' quickly.
- If you can refrain from judgement, you will find they listen more and will also respect the relationship more. They will also come to you earlier in the challenge in the future.
- Ensure your strategies and advice work—don't make it up. That's okay, you won't. It's not your style and you couldn't bear to give advice that wasn't correct!

Investor warning

In my experience, when people are contracting their Greatness and going into breakdown, this role is one of the first to be dropped. People in breakdown don't want reality and will almost always reject practical advice and support. They make YOU the cause of their problems and blame you for their breakdown. Many sever the relationship with the Grounder as they can't handle reality when they are in breakdown. My suggestion to you is to LOVE them anyway, not take it personally, and be open and available when they have worked it all out, knowing that sometimes that may never happen. Remember, you create a critical perspective that keeps everything in balance and it may be a thankless, unappreciated contribution you make.

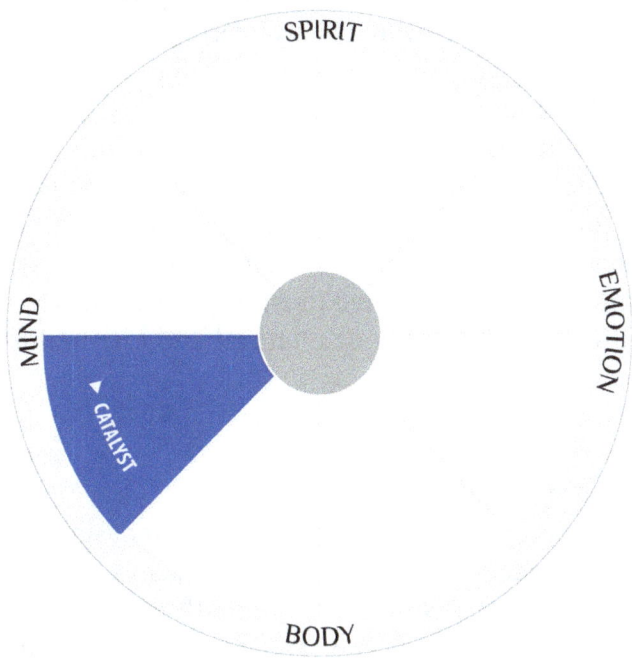

Catalyst: incitement, challenge, growth

i. Just by being yourself (however that is), you INCITE your subject to take certain actions and to experience certain feelings. The impact of those actions and feelings is extremely powerful on your subject. They are usually negative and really, at the end of the day, it doesn't really matter to you. You are not usually directly affected by their actions or feelings.

ii. You CHALLENGE your subject to expand and grow as a human being. When you are around, the status quo is shaken and your subject has to step up to the challenge you naturally create. Don't worry, you don't have to sit for hours thinking of a challenges for your subject. They will just show up in a conversation, a statement, a comment, something you do or something you don't do that will have a profound effect on them. It may surprise you as you were just being yourself, doing what you do best and all of a sudden they are reacting, in tears of joy, fits of laughter, or yelling, or stomping away from you in anger, cursing your name or avoiding you and you'll be wondering what happened.

iii. When people experience powerful feelings with a challenge to GROW, it's an intense time in their life. GROWTH is change and change is never easy. Your subject will have to make new decisions, acquire new skills, change focus, prioritise and sometimes unlearn what they know. This rapid growth makes them feel extremely vulnerable and a little lost as they are moving into uncharted territory. This is exactly what they need to progress in life. It's natural and essential to achieve Greatness.

How to relate to the Catalyst
- Anyone you have in your life that you cannot stand, hate, have bad vibes about, don't want in your life or can't be with is a Catalyst for you. Accept them and firstly embrace their role for you and then, as fast as you can, accept them in your life. Stop pushing them away: that won't support you.
- When you can accept the Catalyst, and can accept what they incite and challenge in you, you can then grow the skills and take the necessary actions in your life. When you do that, the Catalyst's impact on you diminishes rapidly. If you keep ignoring the Catalyst, you will continually have uncomfortable, powerful feelings and negative thoughts about this person and keep them distant from you.
- A Catalyst can be anybody or anything, from a brand new baby, a boss, a relative, to a local group wanting to save a heritage building! Anyone or anything that you have a strong reaction to … yes, they are a catalyst for you and there is something there for you to learn. Learn it and move on.
- You may find personal development programs useful in understanding yourself more and thus becoming more personally self-aware and therefore understanding your Catalyst more.

How be the Catalyst
- Just be yourself!
- Don't take your subject's reaction to you personally. It's not about you.
- Love your subject, even more than normal. Be empathetic and understanding, yet don't fix anything for them, let them solve the issue themselves.
- If you can see there is an intensity to any of your relationships that's more than normal, accept that you are a Catalyst to that person. It's probably best not to go up to them and tell them you're their Catalyst: they may not appreciate it. Giving them a copy of this book may support them to accept you and your role, or it might aggravate them even more. Smile and breathe! ☺
- Accept that some people never resolve everything in their life, and they may use YOU as the reason/excuse or blame you for their misery. Remember, that's their stuff, it's not your fault and it has nothing to do with you.

Investor warning

When you are a Catalyst, people will either love you or hate you, and that's the way it's supposed to be. However, when a person is in breakdown and contracting their Greatness, it could have started with something you said, or not said, or did or didn't do. Being comfortable is easy and mostly dangerous. When we are comfortable, we don't grow and our strengths diminish over time.

Human beings willingly strive for change to become comfortable as fast as possible.

Know that you will be one of the first people to be dropped from your subject's wheel. If you don't know you're their Catalyst, you won't be able to do much about that. However if you know you're their Catalyst, then don't make them wrong for not engaging with you or for being mad with you. If you can do that (it may be hard sometimes), you've actually done your job. You started a chain reaction for your subject

Chapter 5

that is causing them to grow and develop and you don't actually have to hang around to find out the outcome if you don't want to. If you are friends, lovers, spouses or relatives, this can be a very testing time as you want to stay connected to them. However, we're all here to live, love and learn any way we can and as a wife, parent, son, sister, uncle, friend, grandparent, neighbour etc., sometimes we all need to let the people we care about go off on their own journey to find out who they are and what's important to them. So separation, divorce, estrangement, feuds and other separation behaviour and actions are sometimes necessary and okay. The very nature of a catalyst causes transformation. You can't control the outcome, you have to let it unfold how it will, and love the person anyway. The best thing to do when your subject is in major breakdown is to back off. The transformation is happening and you need to make sure that, if your subject isn't talking to you, they are talking to their other Great8™ Investors as much as possible.

Note: Occasionally you won't know you've been or are a Catalyst for someone. Be okay with that. You might have said, done or not done something you didn't even know about. It might just be you being your beautifully awesome self that has caused a stranger to come up to you and say something that might be a bit weird, aggressive, emotional or confronting. Take a breath and see the bigger picture. The person doing this is growing and learning and it's okay. It is best not to go too deep with them as it's their stuff, and being a bit removed and distant can manage the situation.

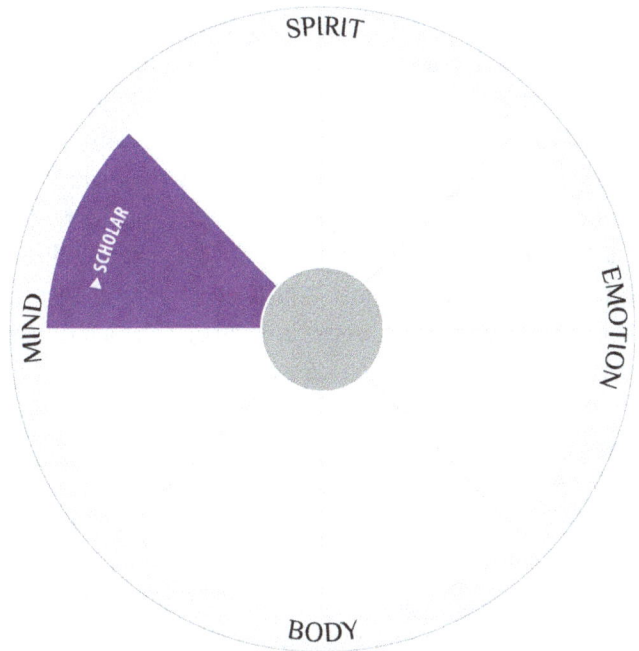

Scholar: ideas, intellect, consequences

i. IDEAS come through thinking and bouncing thoughts with others. The Scholar Investor loves ideas and being creative with their mind with you! They don't have to be overly creative in their life or in any other endeavour to be your strategist. What is important is that when it comes to your conversations with them, they come alive with ideas, strategies and possibilities for you and your hopes and dreams.

ii. The Scholar engages their INTELLECT with you. Their knowledge, archives, reference materials, resources and tools are accessed to support you. What's fabulous about this Investor is that they actively THINK about you and your ideas, circumstances and life as a whole and about how it's going and how it can be better. Just soak that in for a moment. This person gives up their own time to think about YOU and how your life can be better. Such an amazing gift!

iii. Such intense thinking will ultimately identify CONSEQUENCES of actions, choices and behaviour. The Scholar arms you with all the permutations of outcomes from your ideas. Unlike the Grounder, they will not tell you which idea/option you should choose. Actually, after they have explored options with you, they will leave it up to you to choose. Then when you have chosen, they will be right there with you looking at the next lot of options and consequences from that point, just like the satellite navigator in your car. Whatever route you take, they will recalculate the most effective, efficient journey forward. The past doesn't matter to the Scholar as they are focussed on the future and results.

How to relate to the Scholar
- Talk to them early about your ideas and plans.
- Know they will not necessarily have an answer or ideas for you instantly.
- Be ready to capture their ideas and thoughts. The conversation will usually start by them saying, 'I was thinking a lot about what you said about …'
- Be grateful for their time, consideration and sharing, even if you don't agree or like all of what they are saying.
- Don't get too emotional with them too often—it clouds their mind and they are not able to think straight, and that annoys them.
- Do tell them you love and appreciate them: just pick your moment and make sure they really get the message.
- Share results with them. They will LOVE it, as they know they 'hatched the plan' with you.

How to be the Scholar
- Be yourself—any idea or thought is good!
- Any idea you have, write it down or convey it to your subject straightaway through a conversation, phone call or email.
- Do not judge your subject's choice, even if it's a bad one. People have to learn through their own experiences. If you refrain from

judging, they will be open to more conversations with you to get the wider perspective they need before making any more decisions.
- If you haven't heard from your subject in a while, go find them and check they are okay. They need to be talking to you, and if they are not, they might need your support more than either of you realise.

Investor warning

For people who are having success in their life, your role further expands and strengthens their ability and results as they have balance and perspective, and have thought through options and consequences of their chosen path—well done! However, when people are in breakdown, they get overwhelmed by their negative emotions. Know that it will be hard for your subject to stop FEELING and start THINKING.

In tough times you need to have a thick skin and push past their rejection of your wanting to support or be involved in their life. They'll tell you they're okay, they don't need you, things aren't too bad when in actual fact, THAT is the time for you to step it up with them on their options before things get really bad. A subject in total breakdown will have pushed you away. They will make you angry or totally frustrated with them, maybe made you feel used, manipulated or controlled. They are masters at manipulating emotions, and pre-schoolers in using their thinking. You have the ability and skills to flick on their thinking switch. Focus on their highest values (career, family, business, health, or finances, whatever they value most) and show them the consequences if they make better choices moving forward. Show them the bigger picture looking brighter in conversation. Also, if you know their Anchor, Sage or Enthusiast Investors, talk to them, as they will be able to back you up and also support your subject to shift from negative emotions to more positive thoughts and actions.

Chapter 5

Corrective Feedback: why it is important for Greatness

One of the roles of the Great8™ is to provide Corrective Feedback to their subject. Corrective Feedback is when a person has a strong trusted relationship with their subject and they offer a genuine, sincere perspective and/or advice to support the subject to improve their performance, understanding, behaviour, interpersonal skills or relationships. The feedback is designed to have the subject test, check and take positive action. It gives the subject the opportunity to SELF-CORRECT.

It's a bit like the autopilot on a plane. As a plane flies 14 hours from Sydney, Australia, to Los Angeles, USA, it's fair to say that the plane is going to be off track most of the time. The autopilot continually takes in little bits of information of things such as wind, thermal patterns, direction, speed, altitude, fuel, weight of the plane, and performance of the plane's engines, and provides corrective feedback to keep the plane in the air and on track, with enough fuel to land.

For Corrective Feedback to be most effective, it must have two elements:

1. It must be REQUESTED. It's your job to ASK your Great8™ Investors for their point of view, thoughts, ideas, criticism and feedback on your situation, circumstances, choices, world perception, options and position. If your Great8™ just come out and give it to you, it's much harder to accept. You've put these people into your Greatness Wheel, now it's your job to seek their perspective and points of view.

2. The Corrective Feedback must be given with sensitivity, with the intention of making a difference and showing that you have your subject's best interests at heart. All of your Great8™ Investors are invested in you, so listen to them from that perspective and if you are the one giving feedback, speak to your subject with love and remind them you are one of their Great8™ and you've got

something you have to tell them that they need to hear. Choose your moment for the best chance of them listening and taking it in. You want them to understand their position, choices, what they have created or the impact of who they are being.

Your Investors have your best interests at heart

Your Great8™ have your best interests at heart. They are invested in YOU, and in a ME-focussed, lone wolf world it's hard to appreciate that some people actually do have your best interests at heart. I thought I'd take a few pages to share what that might look like from each of the Great8™ Investors. Here's an outline of what they might say or do!

Enthusiast
WOW, you are amazing.
I am so inspired by what you are doing and what's happening for you.
What awesome thing have you done recently?
You're incredible, I was telling someone your story about (insert here) the other day.
Go on, tell them the story about (insert here).
I'm so happy to see you.
I'm your biggest fan.
I've got a whole group of people coming along.
I was stuck the other day and I thought to myself, what would YOU do in this situation and I did that, and it worked!
You are the best. I love spending time with you.
Let me pay for coffee, lunch, dinner. It's been so great to hear all about (insert here).

Sage
You've done this before, are you sure this is the right thing for you?
I remember when we were younger, you always wanted to do (insert here). Maybe you should?
I've known you for over (10, 20, 30, 40) years, that's not YOU.

Chapter 5

Okay, now cut the BS and tell me what's really going on.
Don't lie to me, tell me the truth.
You always do that. I can rely on you to be YOU!
I promise to keep this confidential (and yes, trust the Sage, they will).
I'm coming over, you don't sound like yourself.
They organise your other Investors to make contact with you and they keep track of who is in your life.

Motivator
What's it going to take for you to get that done?
Get over yourself, princess.
If you want this so bad, then stop making excuses!
It's going to take action—you've got to do something to get something.
Sitting still will make your mind lazy, your emotions wallow and your body FAT.
I don't care if you don't like me, but when I'm done, you will respect me.
Right, we are going out. Come on, you're coming with me.
They take the food out of your hand, they throw the jacket on your arm in the bin, they take the book out of your hands, they nudge you at a seminar when a notable point is made by the speaker, and they invite you to train with them, go to yoga with them or do something physical with them.

Bystander
I haven't seen you in while. When can we catch up?
I've got time on the weekend, call me.
Good luck with that!
How did you go?
What's happening now?
What's going on for you?
How are the kids?
They show up on your doorstep unannounced and say 'you've been on my mind and I thought I'd pop in and say hi.'

Anchor
You're bigger than this.
I know you can do it.
There's too much at stake for you to fail. I know you won't fail.
I've got your back.
Now is the right time and YOU are the right person to make this happen.
Fight with your back to the wall. You will win, I know it.
Don't give up, you are stronger and better than this.
It's only a setback or a delay, keep going.
I'm not letting you go, I don't care that you think you don't need me.
I'm staying—deal with it.
I am so proud of you.
They show you a scrapbook of all the achievements, photos, medals, milestones they've saved.
They come with you to important meetings, events or ceremonies (or come and wait outside or downstairs or in the car).

Grounder
I want to understand what you are doing right now.
You are in over your head.
Stop being an idiot and start listening.
You are going to get hurt if you keep doing that and its already hurting (insert here).
Show me the money. Show me the details.
This has got to stop NOW.
I don't care if you don't want to speak to me after this, but someone has got to tell you the truth.
You are making a big mistake and if you don't listen it's going to blow up in your face.
You are a narcissist—you are one of the most self-centred people I know.
You've got no idea about the impact you have on others.
They get you to write a list. They make you show them your bank account and records. They demand to see the business plan or the details. They come to your house or your business and walk right in and demand you start talking. They are upfront, bold and they don't care how you feel about them, AND they love you.

Catalyst (negative angle)
Have you finished (insert here) yet? Seems like you're all talk and no action.
You're never going to achieve anything.
You are stupid/wrong/bad/selfish/too caring (insert anything that aggravates you).
That will never work.
No-one will buy/invest/use that.
What education or qualifications do you have to be doing that?
You're not enough and you never will be.
They cancel a project. They withdraw support. They insult you. They hurt your feelings. They are even more blunt and brutal with reality than the Grounder.
They move into your house/business/life and change everything.
They gossip about you or blast something negative about you on social media, which isolates you.
They come into your world and turn it upside down just by being there (baby, blended family, pet).
They leave you though death, divorce or move to another country at short notice.

Catalyst (positive angle)
Here's a huge opportunity and I think you can do it.
Have you ever considered (insert here)? I know it's not your usual thing, however I think you'd be great at it.
Steve Jobs/Oprah/Winston Churchill/Abraham Lincoln (insert someone famous) had the exact same challenge that you face right now—look where they ended up!
Go for it, kid.
Stop listening to everyone else and follow your heart/trust yourself.
They come into your world and turn it upside down just by being there (baby, blended family, pet).
They love you and want to be with you—which pulls you out of isolation.

Scholar
I read your email last week and I'd like to talk to you about it.
You know your plan about (insert here), I've been thinking about it and I'd like to discuss the pros and cons of it before you make a decision.
Have you thought that through?
You know there's more to that than you think. Want to talk?
Have you got a backup? What's your B, C and D plan?
What will be the impact on (insert here) if this works?
What's your next step?
Who's going to help you? Do you have support?
How can this be financed?
What are your options?
Where are you going to invest the profit?
They organise a strategy session or planning meeting, and bring out a whiteboard, flipchart or spreadsheet.

What do the Great8™ get from being involved?

Okay, so the Great8™ are an awesome group of people to have. Again in this ME-centric, lone wolf world I can also appreciate that it might be difficult to see that the Great8™ Investors actually get a RETURN on their investment. Just like the role of an investor in any business, financial or community deal, they get a return. In the case of the Greatness Principle®, each of the Great8™ experience great value from being involved in your life. I've created two columns below. The first one is the return on their investment based on what they give in their role. The second column is the personal benefit they get out of being in the relationship.

Great8™ Investor	Return on Investment	Benefit to Them
Enthusiast	They get inspiration. They can celebrate with you. They get great joy and energy. They get stories to share with others. They feel good. They can shift their mood. They get someone to model/copy. They become more interesting. They have something to focus on, other than themselves. They come out of their world and meet other Enthusiasts of you and your other Great8™ Investors. They get to give willingly and freely all they have to someone who appreciates and wants their gift.	The ability to marvel at life's magnificence and celebrate possibility. It's fun. They feel good. They can use your energy to change their mood, their perspective and their life. They have a beacon of light in their life (you) and to them it's holy. They get to be part of something great and it might be bigger than they could ever create themselves.
Sage	They are a witness to the life of someone who is great. They have a personal relationship that is deep and meaningful. They learn how to have long-term relationships through their relationship with you. They get a vision/hope for the human race by being in relationship with you. They are an expert and/or trusted advisor on a subject they know really well—YOU.	They are connected to you. They get a soul connection. They are deeply invested in a person other than themselves. They learn acceptance, patience, practice non-judgement and see life and all its glory, drama and beauty through you. They share their wisdom with others through the collection of knowledge and experiences they have learned through watching your life.

Great8™ Investor	Return on Investment	Benefit to Them
Motivator	They get to be involved at the ground level and support you to do what's got to be done. They are able to take the credit for getting you into action and being accountable. They feed off the buzz of being in action and following passion. It fuels them and inspires them to do it with others.	They know themselves to be someone who causes results. They are creators and high-ego people and your results feed their ego and reinforce their identity. They share your strategies and results with others they are motivating. They use all proved strategies and tactics and love having a huge knowledge base to smash any barrier or obstacle to get the results!
Bystander	They get perspective for their own life and learn your lessons from your life without having to go through what you did. They get information and knowledge about other domains they haven't invested in or learned about. They experience non-judgement and total acceptance. They have fun and enjoy the interaction.	They get time out from their world. They get to be with another person who's disconnected from their world. They walk away appreciating their own life and circumstances more than they did before talking with you. They get the opportunity to change their life or have the courage to do something different or copy what you've done, knowing it can work.

Chapter 5

Great8™ Investor	Return on Investment	Benefit to Them
Anchor	They love you so much, they want you to be happy and successful. When you are, they are deeply proud and eternally happy. They have a deep, soul relationship that defines who they are for themselves and others. They get the experience of knowing themselves as a stayer, a solid reliable, committed person. They are the champion of hope and possibility for you and the people around them.	They experience making a difference. They get out of themselves and are there, completely present with/for another person. They see possibility for themselves through their conversations with you and the actions you take. They share your stories of challenge and triumph to inspire others and also relive the whole experience, as it makes them feel so good to relive and re-tell it.
Grounder	The get to tell it like it is. They get to be themselves without being judged, attacked or resented. They get to be right. They are, in this instance, an authority/expert. They get to problem solve and be a bit forensic, digging through the facts. They genuinely want to make a contribution to your life and you let them give what they have. They feel validated.	They get respect and appreciation from you. Others don't give them that. They don't get the usual resistance and pushback from you. They get to see you implementing changes and suggestions they have given you.

Great8™ Investor	Return on Investment	Benefit to Them
Catalyst	They get to be themselves.	It's fun and a bit naughty. They love it.
	They don't have to be polite, correct, appropriate or nice.	They get to break rules, challenge the status quo and be different.
	They have permission to be controversial and antagonistic.	They don't have to put up with BS, they can cut through your stories and get to the core.
	They get to shake everything up on purpose.	
	They have permission to stretch, grow and challenge you any way they think would benefit you.	They experience themselves to be a bit of a renegade in life, even if it's only with you.
	They can be creative and express themselves freely to create an impact, an effect or get a reaction.	
Scholar	They get to have meaningful discussions and conversations.	They love thinking and strategising.
	They use a lot of brain power to problem solve.	This activity keeps them alert.
		This activity excites and energises them.
	It keeps them sharp.	It's fun.
	It expands their own knowledge base and experience, which is something they value highly.	They feel important.
		They feel they are making a significant contribution.
	They get to try out strategies and solutions without having to do it themselves or take on any risk.	They feel more normal as they don't meet many people who think like they can and do.
	Their ideas and strategies are validated and taken.	They can use any idea or strategy that works for themselves or with others.

Chapter 5

Don't let anyone else be a reason for your mediocrity. Be great and they will either come with you, or step aside.
~ Jen Harwood

Chapter 6

The First Investor™

The Greatness Principle® will only work when YOU CHOOSE to be better than your circumstances and have decided that you've had enough of the pain, drama, heartache and mediocrity of your life. You are the First Investor™ in your life and it's your job to invest in yourself on many levels and acknowledge and invite your Great8™ into your world.

Stop looking down at the ground in despair and start to look up. Who is around you? Who is trying to support you? Who is offering support that you are turning away, ignoring, brushing off or can't even hear? These people are your life ring. They hold you up and allow you to steer, drive and move around in life.

Stop waiting for your life to change. Change it yourself—NOW.

Stop blaming others for what they've done or are doing. Wallowing in it or choosing to stay in it creates absolutely NOTHING. In fact, let me correct that, it doesn't create something—it creates more of it.

If you are suffering anything in your life, you've got to say something to someone who has your best interests at heart and then do something about it, with them supporting you. Suffering is a choice, and before you sit there and say 'Jen, you don't know about my problem, my suffering, my situation ...', I'm going to say this to you ...

I watched my mother, Cath, when she was incredibly sick with cancer, endure horrific side effects and pain for seven years and NOT ONCE did she suffer in it. She chose her situation, got support to manage and deal with it as best she could to have an incredible life living with cancer. She learned new skills, she started public speaking, and she was one of the most revered cancer survivors on the global internet cancer chat forums, giving advice and support to people all over the world. She participated in the Living Books program in Bendigo.

http://www.abc.net.au/local/videos/2008/11/28/2432729.htm

Every time she left the house for an 'adventure', she would end up bailed up on the couch for days afterwards, paying the physical price for the exertion. She didn't suffer, she knew the consequences of her actions, she had pain management support and carried with her enough morphine patches and morphine lollipops to put any of us into a coma.

Cath powerfully chose her vision over her circumstances. Yes, I even did this with my mum when she was about 18 months into cancer and chemo. She created a vision board of how she wanted her life to be, knowing she was going to die. Her vision was 'to live and love fully, to learn and experience as much of the world as I can, until I can't!' Come on, think about the alternative to her vision—a miserable existence of suffering all the way to death. She lived that vision and more all the way to the end.

Okay, so you've lost all your money, your business has failed, your wife/husband has left you, you've been convicted of a crime, you are in prison, you are addicted to hard drugs, your child has died, your loved ones have died, you've suffered a horrific injustice, you've been excommunicated from your family or group, your parents were cruel, you've suffered abuse, you've got a terminal illness or have a physical, mental or emotional disability and you can't walk, or half your face is droopy from a stroke, or you look different or you're fat, anorexic, bulimic or you've just been having a bad day for weeks, months or years ...

STOP! You've forgotten the MOST important thing in life.

YOU ARE ALIVE AND YOU ARE HERE TO LIVE.

Your life won't be GREAT if you continually suffer and isolate yourself, withdraw from the world and aren't investing in yourself. Complaining, moaning and replaying the stories, the dramas and the hardship is just boring after you've said it a few times, and for the people listening, it's really boring when you just keep going on and on about it and how unfair life is.

Get clear on the facts

It's time to shake yourself out of this vicious cycle. YOU have to interrupt it and change your focus and direction. You've got to get clear with where you are right now. Many people in breakdown don't want to look at the bills or demand notices, they don't answer the phone or check emails and they don't look at reality. These types of activities keep you in denial and, more importantly, dig you deeper into your breakdown.

First things first. The easiest way to get clear on the facts is to create a list like the one below. When we are in breakdown, we are being run by our emotions and our most dominant thoughts, which will be mostly negative. The worksheet below will help you to identify quickly where and how you are stuck.

Begin with the first two columns: Problems/Issues are usually thoughts you have that are in a rut and you are not able to bring perspective or creativity to them. Your feelings anchor you in inertia or perpetual drama. The last two columns, Action and Who Can Support don't have to be complete. It's okay if you don't know the action or who can support you yet—we'll get to that shortly. So when you are completing the first two columns, be really honest with yourself. If you don't, you'll most likely leave out a critical problem or issue that will undermine your future greatness. It is best to get it all out now.

First Step		Second Step	
The Problem/Issue	How I feel about it right now	Action to resolve	Who can support me

If you aren't capable of doing this by yourself as you feel completely overwhelmed by your situation and circumstances, then ask one of your Great8™ Investors to support you. When you write the list, don't judge it, don't try to fix it, and don't get depressed about it. Remember, it's just a list, and when everything is dealt with, you will feel much better and you will be back on the road to being great.

Clean up the past

You do not wake up one morning a bad person. It happens by a thousand tiny surrenders of self-respect to self-interest.
~ Robert Brault, http://www.robertbrault.com/

So face it, you've got a few, if not lots of mistakes and mess ups. Congratulations, you are HUMAN. There is no need to get really upset or dramatise your list. You can't be Great if you still have mistakes and mess ups along the way that haven't been addressed and/or completed. Now, I'm not saying you have to fix everything in your past: sometimes that's not possible and not the best choice. What is required is that YOU are at peace with the past so it no longer runs you or your life. If you are not at peace with your past, then you will be making decisions and choices that are affected by the past and not moving forward. It will be the experience of same day, different circumstances, same solutions, no progress, more frustration.

Cleaning up the past—paying bills, saying sorry, finally doing something that you said you would do, fulfilling a promise, cleaning up a mess, stopping something that others have repeatedly asked you to do and yet you haven't etc.—sets you free and also lightens your load of breakdown. You get back into INTEGRITY and start to get energy, inspiration and momentum. So the place to start is with little steps, little actions to get the momentum going. Pick anything you can do immediately to fix any of the problems you've listed. There may be some 'no-brainers' that you could do right away. Do them and remember that sometimes fixing one problem/issue will solve some of the others at the same time.

Tell the truth

You can now approach and talk to your Great8™. It is essential to remember before you do that all of your Investors love you, support you and want the best for you. They have your best interests at heart.

To be able to support you they need to know the truth about what you are dealing with. That's why you've written your list. I know from personal experience that sharing the reality and the truth about my situation and position in life was really hard, and I almost didn't do it. If you have trouble saying what needs to be said, give them the list first and, I promise you, the conversation will go from there.

There is no rule about the order of Great8™ Investors you share with. I suggest you follow your intuition and start with someone who will be supportive and empowering—probably not your Catalyst! When you are ready to share your list and your current reality, let your Investor know beforehand that you've got something important to speak with them about and that you may need a couple of hours. When telling the truth, it's hard to do it in ten minutes as the other person will want to ask questions and you will want to explain stuff. So it is best that they are in a position where they don't have to rush off from what they thought was the quick-coffee-and-catch-up session you usually do, or, if you usually meet your Great8™ Investor at work, from a public place or their home with their family present: organise to go to a quieter place where you won't be disturbed.

Why Bother?—the assassin of Greatness

Why Bother is going to be the most dominant thought or state of mind you are going to be up against. When in breakdown, everything seems hopeless, lost, too hard, too … everything. You must realise that saying or thinking *Why Bother* is your number one enemy.

When you say or think *Why Bother,* you are: giving up your great future, accepting mediocrity or less, being ordinary, being a child (a spoilt brat, even), being irresponsible and a genuine loser. **If you say or think *Why Bother,* then you are an assassin of Greatness.** I don't apologise to you for writing this. You've got to understand that *Why Bother* is a poisonous mix of resignation and cynicism, and it will slowly and painfully kill you and everything you love and that is most important to you.

Why Bother stops you from taking action, stops you taking responsibility, stops you fixing problems/issues, and also lets other people's actions, behaviours and words affect you and your environment negatively. *Why Bother* excuses them and anchors everyone else to not seek or believe in Greatness. *Why Bother* is such a simple phrase: it sounds innocent enough, yet it is deadly!

If you take one action out of this section of the book, I urge you to remove the phrase *Why Bother* out of your mind and vocabulary immediately and replace it with *I care because ...* or *This is important because ...* These phrases get you out of your pity party and back into reasons to act and move forward that are bigger than just you.

You can make a choice right now that will change the entire direction of your life. List all the reasons why you care about having a great life, business, family, marriage, career, home, community. I'll bet most of your reasons aren't actually for YOU. This list will support you prepare for daily living.

Let me give you an example. My husband, Simon, promised me that he'd be home every night for the next two weeks at 4 pm so that I could take the time I needed to write the rest of this book. He's one of my Great8™ and he loves and supports my work, however in the last week, he managed to come home by 4 pm only once, so I had one night to work on the book and the rest of the week I cared for our baby daughter with dinner, bath and bed routines (which I totally enjoyed). Yet, deep down, I was angry, frustrated and annoyed and **I could have gone into the place of** *why bother* asking for his support, he doesn't really care about my work, his work is more important than mine, I can't rely on him, I can't get done what I need to get done, it's all too hard, being a mum and a business woman is too hard. What's the point, we are all suffering, why bother asking him to do anything for me, why bother writing a book, why bother at all!

Now, in the past the old me would have gone there and even picked a fight with Simon, which would have affected our marriage, the communication flow and upset everything, even the peace and love in the house for our daughter. However, I realised his actions demonstrated one thing to me … he didn't care enough to keep his promise because … **my vision wasn't big enough and unmessable.** I wasn't fully committed to a vision that touched, moved and inspired me. That's it. He's not wrong, he's not at fault, I was. It was a bitter pill to swallow and, to my relief, Simon didn't point it out and make me wrong for blaming him. If I wanted the result I had to ask myself the fundamental questions:

1. What am I committed to that's bigger than me?
2. What am I prepared to do?
3. What is it going to take to make it happen?
4. Who can support me to make it happen?
5. What are the barriers I have to deal with to still get the job done?

I drew up a wheel for this book and started to see who THIS PROJECT's Great8™ were. To my surprise and delight, there were Investor roles vacant. I needed to identify who the book needed to make it GREAT. I've got them now: they are on board, and guess what … the book's flowing. I've miraculously got time to write it and get it done. Hey, it's in your hands right now!

Why didn't it get done in the last five years? Because I was so arrogant about myself and my life that I was playing a very small game. I gave up thinking I could do it by myself, and used lots of reasons (my mum died), excuses (I moved states), distractions (I got married), circumstances (I had no support), and justifications (I had a new baby) why it wasn't done.

Upon reflection, the first book I ever wrote, *The Art of Networking*, had lots of people supporting me. It was a great success, because I had my Great8™ working with me. Yes, I had become a Lone Wolf and was again trying to do everything by myself!

So what's not Great in your life?

Where in your work, business and/or life are you struggling right now and not talking about it to anyone?

Where are you suffering in silence?

What's it going to take for you to get over yourself and start letting others throw you a life ring of support?

Is your vision just a nice to have or a MUST HAVE?

Why are you messing around being small, mediocre and boring?

Boundary management

The other things you must focus on for yourself are your BOUNDARIES. Having coached so many people, I know the biggest issue they all face is managing boundaries and expectations, and keeping themselves and others accountable. If your life is in breakdown, I can assure you that YOU have collapsed your boundaries and compromised your own rules about what is okay and what is not. Now, I have done this myself over the years, let others come into my world thinking they would respect me and step gently in my life. They didn't. They stomped all over the place and flattened me, my confidence and my will to be great. Does that sound familiar for you or someone you know?

If that's the case, the first thing to do is to accept that YOU let them come in and YOU didn't manage the boundaries about what was okay and not okay. I needed professional people to support me in understanding how, when and why I would compromise my own boundaries. This was awesome and totally liberating. I got a new level of personal awareness and could hold my own ground and allow others to take responsibility for their actions. I'd learned how to stop over-supporting, over-managing and taking responsibility for others, in the name of 'helping' them.

Chapter 6

An example of that was when I was in a relationship early in my life with my boyfriend, Bill. He regularly went out with the boys after work and would sometimes come to my place drunk. The first time it was funny, then the second time he did, it was stupid and the third time it was annoying. So, I created the new boundary that being drunk in my home was unacceptable and not tolerated. Bill agreed to this boundary and promised not to visit me when he was drunk.

It was a week after this agreement was made and at about 9 pm I heard a lot of laughter outside the block of flats where I was living. I looked out the window and saw a police car, and Bill was standing next to it with a policeman. I went downstairs to see what was going on.

Bill had been escorted home (to my place) by the police. The officer smiled at me and said, 'Don't worry, love, he's done nothing wrong. I saw him walking on the street and thought it best I bring him home.' I was livid with anger and said to myself, 'Done nothing wrong? He's drunk and he's going to come in. I don't think so, he knows the rules!'

The officer left and Bill stood there trying to focus on anything that was standing still. WHAT was I going to do with him? How was I going to hold my boundary? I had a discussion with him (as best you can with a drunk person) and told him he had broken the rules. He dismissed it with a laugh and said, 'Oh Jen, I know, don't worry, I'll sleep here on the footpath. I've been a bad, bad boy, I know.' He lay down on the footpath and closed his eyes.

Far out! What to do? I called one of my Great8™ Investors. She told me that he would wake up soon and be cold and would come inside because he had the keys. I had to get his keys so he couldn't come in. The other thing she said to me was, 'Jen, if you take his keys, are you prepared for the worst case scenario of him trying to cross the road to get to the park bench or grass and him being run over and injured or killed? Are you prepared for that?'

What a question. I hated that question. I was angry, and I wanted to hold my boundary. She had made me see both sides of the coin and allowed me to choose for myself. I said yes. So, I went back downstairs and took the keys from him. As I did, he'd forgotten he'd already talked to me and how he got home so we went through the bad boy and taking keys conversation all over again.

I went upstairs and waited. Thirty minutes later, the buzzer went. He wanted to come inside and he had 'lost' his keys. I told him that I had his keys and he couldn't come in. Again we had a long discussion about this and he finally understood that I wasn't letting him in. My Great8™ Investor warned me that he could get angry, violent, kick the door down, and make a huge fuss. Was I prepared to call the police? Yes. Luckily, Bill understood the situation. He knew he'd broken our agreement.

Then another half an hour went by and there was a knock on the flat door. He had managed to come in with neighbours coming home from eating dinner out. They let him in. So he was now at my door, and a little bit more sober. I texted him and said, 'if you don't stop knocking, I will call the police'. The texts went back and forth. His texts were starting to make sense and I nearly opened the door. Then, the texts suddenly stopped. I was relieved, he'd finally got the message. I went to bed. What I didn't know was that his phone battery had gone flat and he ended up sleeping in the stairwell.

The next morning at 6 am there was a knock on the door. It was Bill. I opened the door and looked at him. He was a mess. Hung-over, smelly, dishevelled and looking sad, guilty, ashamed and hoping for forgiveness. I grabbed him by his shirt collar, pulled him to me and kissed him fully and then said, 'I love you, and I don't love that behaviour. You knew the rules and you broke them.' He burst into tears and told me that I had done the right thing by not letting him in. I can tell you it was a hard night AND I'd held a boundary with Bill who, up until that point, I had let break lots of them. I had honoured MY word and I was honouring ME. I felt strong. I felt more in control of my life and I felt that I had the ability to manage my boundaries better with him and in other areas of my life.

Where have you let your boundaries drop? Where have you caved in and now have a situation that is totally off track, out of control or going in a direction that's wrong for you? Remember, YOU have let your boundaries be trampled. If you have people not honouring your boundaries, you have to fix it. My example with Bill worked for me. It might not work for you. Talk to your Great8™ Investors about your situations and challenges and hatch a plan to re-establish your boundaries and rules for honouring your life.

How to be the First Investor™ to yourself

- Greatness starts with you. Create a Vision of the life and results you want.
- Take responsibility for your life and your current situation.
- Work on your character and start to honour your word and commitments.
- Stop any destructive addictions and habits immediately and if you can't do it by yourself, get professional support NOW. Don't wait, just do it.
- Remember, you are the guardian of your own life. Manage your boundaries and enforce and teach people your rules and values!
- Nurture, develop and protect your self-esteem. Be around people who are uplifting, inspiring and generous. Remove yourself from environments, situations and people that are negative, degrading and offensive.
- Remember, many will tell you what to do, however the only person who can take responsibility for your life and take action is YOU.
- Be loving to yourself. Get sleep, time out, take holidays, read books, do what you love.
- Celebrate achievements and milestones. Celebrate being you and being alive.

- Be grateful for all you have every day—even the not so good days—they make you better.

Investor warning

The last 30 years have seen a massive development in the personal development industry with self-help books, courses, programs and activities for the individual to 'work on themselves to be better'. Having worked with the best personal development gurus of the 20th and 21st centuries such as Tony Robbins, John Demartini, Brandon Bays, Dr Bruce Lipton, and Carolyn Myss, as well as done extensive training with Landmark Education, Thomas Leonard, and CoachU, I believe that it's a given that we will all be working on ourselves for the rest of our lives.

I strongly suggest that you take the wisdom from each teacher and guru and apply it, then live and learn some more. We will never be 'perfect' as we are constantly evolving and adapting into better versions of ourselves, every second of every day.

Note: When you work on yourself all by yourself, your learning, progress and character development will be slow and take many months or even years to progress. As challenging as it may be, you MUST be in a relationship with others and start using the Greatness Wheel. Start one Great8™ Investor at a time until your Greatness Wheel is full. Your Great8™ will fast track your awareness, your experiences and insight.

Chapter 6

Repeat after me …
'Being human means that I am capable of being great
and it also means that it is inevitable that
in my quest for greatness I will make mistakes and
mess up along the way.'
~ Jen Harwood

Chapter 7

Greatness Principle® rules

There are eight unbreakable rules when you are working with the Greatness Principle®. You need to know these to make it work.

1. Choose one Domain at a time

I have worked the Greatness Wheel with many of my clients, and it is tempting to look at one's life overall and do a wheel for the general picture. That's how I initially did it with people, but it wasn't anywhere nearly as powerful as when you focus on a specific area or DOMAIN.

A Domain is an area of life that you have declared is important to you and you want to experience Greatness in it. Domains are any areas where we invest time, money and energy. Examples of domains are your business/company, career, marriage, parenting, family, health, sport, hobbies, school, church, community, special projects, charity etc.

Chapter 7

Choose the Domain and then, looking at your life, focus on that Domain and look to see who you already have that's supporting you in that Domain. For example, I chose to apply the Greatness Principle® to the Domain of Motherhood. In October 2010, my mother died from cancer. I was nine weeks pregnant at the time and I realised that the usual support I'd get going into my own motherhood journey would be missing my Sage. I was concerned, yet not too worried. Then, when I was a few months pregnant, we moved to Sydney—away from my current circle of friends and support. I was working and had people I knew around me, but when I ended up having the baby I came home from hospital and I was there alone. My husband, Simon, went back to work within two weeks and my sister Kate (who had left her own two small children at home in Adelaide with her husband to support me like our mother would have if she were alive), had to go back to her family. I was alone, trying to figure out breastfeeding, being with an infant, and having occasional visits from the midwife. I realised that I needed to build my wheel of support or I'd be in trouble. So I looked at who I had and who was missing in the Domain of me being a GREAT MOTHER!

The wheel above was the Greatness Wheel for the Domain of Mother. I had five of my Great8™. Not enough. I needed to do something.

I had been getting calls from the local health service offering a mothers' group for women who'd had babies within the same six-week period who lived locally. I initially didn't want to go, but I realised I needed to find a Bystander, a Motivator and a Scholar. So off I went, looking for certain people I could connect with. Lucky me, I found two mothers who I really liked and clicked with in the first meeting.

The first one was Sally, mother of Jamilla. She became my brand new Motivator. Sally was into everything about motherhood and researched everything. She'd send me information on events, expos and articles, as well as new parks and playgrounds she'd been to. Sally lived around the corner from me and she'd come by with Jamilla in her baby wrap and off we'd go, taking our bubs for a walk. Sally got me moving and out and about.

Then there was Ashley, mother of Oliver. My brand new Bystander. Ashley is a beautiful woman who had distinct views and opinions about motherhood and what her son would and would not be exposed to, and was very clear about what she was doing and why. She didn't put her opinions on anyone else. In fact, I had to sometimes coax her to tell me what she thought about immunisation, breastfeeding, attachment parenting and other controversial mothering topics. I loved talking to her. We'd share our experiences, views and thoughts and fears. I now had a connection with another mother who shared similar values and vision to me. We remained independent in our own worlds and yet deeply connected as we valued each other's style, information and approach.

So now, I was one investor away from realising Greatness in my mothering. Due to finding Sally and Ashley, by the fourth month of our babies' growth, I was very happy, confident and settled with the change of life and 24/7 baby routine. I loved it. Then, when Rose was one year old, I started to struggle about what to teach my baby and figure out how much to teach, what to teach and how best to do it. The care and nurturing I had all sorted and I was confident in what I was doing. I knew I needed a Scholar for the next bit. Before my mum died, she made me promise to find a mother further down the track with older kids to give me advice, direction and support. I needed that mother now. So I decided to go find my Scholar as a matter of urgency.

I went to any seminar I could get to, with or without my baby. I even gatecrashed a seminar in Ryde and haggled with the lady at the nametag table to let me in (how could she refuse a mother with a baby wanting to learn about parenting!). Then one day, I attended a free session at an Under 3 Montessori Program where mums and bubs went for two hours. The children in this room were from Rose's age up to 18 months old. They were sitting at a little table on little chairs with a placemat, plate, fork and tiny glass and these toddlers were not making a mess. They were eating at the table and doing all sorts of activities that blew my mind. I was engaged and baby Rose was totally engaged. I applied to attend and we were accepted.

In the very first class, the children took off their shoes, socks and pants so they were just in nappies and a shirt so they could feel the ground fully with their feet and legs. Parents were requested to sit back on the stools and NOT engage, talk to their child or give them any eye contact or encouragement whatsoever. We were to allow the child to naturally explore whatever they wanted with no input from us. This was hard for me and I did something not in the rules, and the Directress, Ferne van Zyl, one of Australia's leading Montessori experts, snapped at me and told me to get back to my stool and to let my child figure it out. She said me that, if I wanted an independent, well-adjusted child, I needed to create a relationship that was solid, strong and present. This would allow my child to know she was supported and that she could be herself, not a projection of me. I was stunned and shocked, and immediately loved this woman. I moved back to my stool and, as I did, tears streamed down my face. Ferne was my new Scholar. She knew the mother I wanted to be and she was very happy to give me direction and strategies on how to get there and I was very happy to be given every piece of advice she had to give.

Me with gorgeous Rose

At the time of writing, Rose is now three years old and she is a GREAT child and everyone says I'm a Great mother. Over the last three years, the people in my Greatness Wheel have changed slightly: however, all the people in my wheel have guided, supported, encouraged, challenged, celebrated, watched, strategised and been with me the whole way. I am Great in the Domain of Motherhood and young Rose is the evidence of that.

Under 3yrs Montessori Program

2. The Great8™ must be alive

The people in your Greatness Wheel must be alive. Having first-hand experience of having one of my Great8™ die, I can assure you that to be Great in any Domain and life in general, you need the role of the person who has died to be re-filled. My mother Cath was my Sage. I miss her as my mother and I miss her as my Sage. I can run the emotional files, memories and her words of advice in my mind about what she would say to me in certain situations and circumstances, however your Great8™ need to be able to give you corrective feedback. That means it's interactional and responsive. Running memories in your mind is just a general playback of the past and not interactive. To get interactive, I guess you could go to a clairvoyant, but you will be interacting through the clairvoyant, who is alive. It is best to re-fill the role with a living person who has your best interests at heart, one with whom you can have an interactive relationship. So, as hard as it was for me to accept that my mother was dead, I decided to honour her fully and re-fill the roles in the Domains in my life that Cath had invested in.

3. Great8™ Investors must wait to be asked for corrective feedback to achieve maximum effect

As a Great8™ Investor, you care about your subject. You want them to achieve great success in the Domain they are focussed on, so your job is to support them. Just as we let toddlers stumble and bump around a bit, so too do you have to let your subject stumble and bump and make mistakes. It's all about allowing them to learn and grow and work it out for themselves. Any learning an individual can discover themselves, they will own for the rest of their life. If your subject is experiencing a lot of drama, stay close to them by visiting, calling or emailing or all of these. If you are 'there' with them, they will ask for your support. You can also ask questions that will encourage a request for support from them. What I mean by that is that, if you ask these types of questions, you will start a conversation of self-discovery that may, and I stress may, have them ask for your perspective. You might need to have several conversations until they are ready to share and ask what you think. Be patient and sit back on your stool and WATCH!

Here are some things that you might say to your subject.
Tell me more about that?
What's going on with (insert here)? I thought it was going well.
That's gotta hurt. Does it?
What are you doing about this?
What other options do you have?

How have you managed to cope like this for so long?
Are you talking to anyone about this?
What can I do to support you?
What are the impacts of (insert here) on you? How does it affect others?
How long do you think you can keep doing this?
Do you love it?
How do you feel about all of that?
What do you need right now?
What have you learned?
What are you still yet to learn about all of this?
How do you see it?
What's your point of view about all of that?
Can you help me understand the situation better?

4. You must have one person in one role only

This is very important. When you do a wheel for the first time, people sometimes put one person in two, three or four spots in the wheel, wanting to have it full. I had a lady in a seminar do just this and she said that her husband was four of the roles in her Greatness Wheel. That's not a good idea for a number of reasons:

1. Her husband was four of the eight. If something happened to him, she would automatically lose four roles in her wheel, creating instability and risk for her and her family.
2. Effectively, her husband was over-supporting her. He had four roles to fulfil. That's too much. When people do more than one role for someone else, they don't pay attention to their own wheel and their own Greatness and they start to get out of balance.
3. Over-supporting can lead to resentment, burn out and a lack of appreciation. That in itself will cause a breakdown in the relationship and affect both people in a negative way.
4. We need all of the Great8™ roles filled with different people as all the roles have different perspectives, ideas and qualities to contribute to you. With someone doing double, triple or quadruple roles, you

reduce the diversity of resources, attributes and wisdom available to you.

It is essential that, if you have a person in more than one role, you pick the role they naturally fill best for you, and then declare the other roles that they filled vacant and go find people to fill them. You will be better off, they will be relieved of their over-supporting and have more time to invest in others and spend time with their own Great8™.

5. You don't need to know about the Greatness Principle® for it to work

The Greatness Wheel is for you. It is your responsibility to fill the roles in your life and you actually don't need to let people know you are interacting with them for a reason. If you choose your Great8™ people well, the relationship will work for them and they will really value the relationship and enjoy being with you. I do think it's a good idea to share the Greatness Principle® and this book with them as they may have Domains that aren't as great as they'd like them to be and could use a strategy about how to fix it.

Keeping the Greatness Principle® quiet works especially well with people who are in massive breakdown and are having a very hard time, and YOU are the Great8™ Investor. I don't advise waltzing into someone's life and declaring that you are going to be their Sage or Motivator or Grounder because they need one! They will probably ask you to leave or not to do it because they don't want it, don't understand it or are such a lone wolf that they can't comprehend that someone cares so much about them and wants to support. No, don't declare it: just be it and do it.

I did this for my sister Kate in 2007 when I first moved to Bendigo. My relationship with my sister was close, just not super close. She was in her late 30s, had broken up from her boyfriend, and had decided

Chapter 7

to sell her house in Adelaide and move to Melbourne. So Kate had re-established her life in a new city with her dog and made some new girlfriends and she was getting by. Her life wasn't great, but it was okay. Looking at her life, she had five out of eight of the Great8™ in place. As I wasn't close to her at that point, I knew I needed a closer relationship to support her and be her Grounder. She didn't have one of those in her life.

So I went and found some new business clients to coach in Melbourne (two hours' drive from my house). I asked Kate if I could stay overnight when I came to work with my clients. My sister is one of the most generous people I know. She said sure, she cut me a key to her house and made sure there was food in the fridge I liked. When Kate came home from work, I supported her in any way she wanted. If she wanted her computer fixed, I did it. If she wanted to walk the dog, we went. Whatever Kate wanted to watch on TV, I watched it. I didn't really watch much TV and didn't really want to do that, but I wanted to get into Kate's world and understand what was going on for her. I also wanted her to trust me more and realise that I did care about her at a very deep level; I just hadn't been able to show her for a long time as we lived so far away from each other. So I watched her shows. It was actually fun and made me laugh. After about six months of weekly visits and seeing every episode of Sex in the City a couple of times at least, Kate started to share with me how she felt about her life, her work and her relationships with her friends.

One of Kate's new girlfriends was being Kate's Motivator, but I didn't think she had Kate's best interests at heart. Initially she invited Kate to parties to meet new people, which was good for Kate, being in a new city. Then she wanted Kate to come with her to help meet guys, playing mixed netball, and then dumped her and the team when she found one, which left Kate on her own. I didn't like this girl. She was spending lots of time with Kate and started claiming that their relationship was like sisters. That made me mad: she was not Kate's sister, I was. I've known Kate all her life and I knew her better than this new girl did. I wanted Kate to see the reality of what this girl was doing and how she was hurting Kate. Knowing the rules of being a Greatness Investor, I couldn't tell Kate how I felt about this girl until … Kate asked me. I was hanging out for that moment, and it was really hard to wait.

Then, one day when we were in the car driving to the shops, Kate was talking to me about what this friend did on the weekend and Kate was angry and hurt. When we pulled up at a red light, Kate turned to face me and said, 'Jen, what do you think I should do?' In that moment, I knew Kate trusted me and this was my opportunity to tell her exactly what I thought of this girl and the impact it had on Kate. I told her that she should stop spending time with this girl and that she should make a plan on how to get what she really wanted in life (a husband, kids and a lovely home were what she wanted most). Kate loved what I had to say and she took it all in.

A week later, when I was visiting again, Kate declared that she'd 'broken up' with her friend. I was so happy for her. Then she asked me what I thought about how and where to start getting the life she really wanted instead of treading water in Melbourne. Kate was on her way to Greatness. She was in action. She was alive with excitement and she had given herself permission to create the vision of having her own family. There's a book to be written for sure on what she did and how she did it, however, to cut a long story short, at the time of writing, Kate is married to her lovely husband and together they have two gorgeous children who are now eight and six years old. Kate has her GREAT FAMILY, which is what she's secretly wanted for a very long time, and I am so happy that I was part of her 'unknown' Great8™, supporting her to have it.

6. The Substitute Investor

There are times in life when you are going to lose one of your Great8™. They might die, go into breakdown themselves, not be able to invest, get sick, move away, or the relationship between you ends for a variety of reasons. So, you can have someone else in your wheel fill one other role for a short-term solution. I call them the Substitute Investor. Just like a substitute teacher at school, they aren't there long and hold the fort temporarily until the permanent teacher comes back.

Most people reach out to their spouse or partner or someone else in their Great8™ wheel to fill this role. It's best that they are asked to support you in the additional role and that they agree. Expecting your spouse or loved one to fill a role automatically because it's vacant isn't a good strategy. Doing that puts unnecessary pressure and expectation for them to over-support you. It's much better if it's done by choice rather than guilt or obligation. If one of your Great8™ agrees to temporarily fill another support role for you, excellent. Remember, the general rule of thumb is to not let it go longer than six weeks. Your responsibility while you have the Substitute Investor in place is to find a more permanent person to fill the role. Don't become complacent and comfortable with the substitute. It's not fair for everyone if they keep over-supporting you.

7. The Cloaked Investor™

Cloaked Investors™ are people who are attracted to you because your wheel is filling up. You are out of breakdown and on the up. You are going places and you are happy with yourself and the progress you are making. However, you are still vulnerable. The amount of drama in your life is less than in the past, due to the fact that you have started to re-fill your Greatness Wheel and are taking responsibility for yourself and for your life to be great.

The Cloaked Investor™ is someone who does not have their wheel full at all. Most of the time, they have less than four people in their wheel and they are in breakdown in at least one area of their life. They may not know it, or they are in denial about it. They either pretend or are deluded to think that their life is great.

They have lots of time on their hands as they are experiencing one or more of the following:

- In between jobs
- Just come out of a relationship (short or long term)
- Just relocated to get away from a world of drama
- Closed their business, or walked away from a failing business
- They've been caring for someone who's finally died
- They've been in an abusive or violent situation that's still not over
- They have been on their own for a really long time.

They see you in full flight and brightness, and decide that, if they had you in their life, their life would be much better or perfect.

How they get into your life is quite subtle ...

- They are very attentive
- They give you lots of time
- They offer to help you
- They get you to talk about yourself
- They offer advice and strategies to assist you
- They help you through tough times.

Really, they are a dream come true. Everyone wants someone to be their personal assistant without having to return the investment. And that's the catch. This relationship is NOT balanced. There is no fair exchange and they begin to make themselves indispensable to the point where they convince you that, one by one, you don't need some of your current Great8™ Investors and that THEY can provide that relationship role for you. Most people won't notice the dropping of one of their Great8™ because the Cloaked Investor™ is so great and attentive and helpful and useful and all over your life that it doesn't seem to matter.

STOP right there! It DOES matter—it matters a LOT.

Chapter 7

To have a great life, you need a variety of ideas, thinking and conversations. You can't get it all from just one person. Your goal is to have at least one person in each role at all times (both good times and tough times). When someone wants to be more to you than one, alarm bells should be ringing. Being Great is all about balance. If someone is being more than one role for you, THEY are not in balance themselves and so will not take care of their own wheel. It's a vicious circle that can get out of hand very fast if you're not paying attention.

When you have a Cloaked Investor™ in your life, you will start to experience drama. They have come into your life with drama (sometimes hidden and covered up, or openly declared). Because they have invested in you (through time, money or resources), they will demand an unfair return on their investment and create a sense of obligation and guilt that you help them. And help them you will … In their drama and issues, you won't see that they need to rebuild their wheel and relationships, because the drama and 'stuff' going on is so full-on and complicated that you'll get swept up in it. When that happens, your Great8™ and even other friends and family in your life will notice your lack of attention to your own life and start to comment that this 'other person' is not good for you or doesn't have your best interests at heart. So many times I have heard the reply to this be …

- 'You don't know them like I do and everything they've done for me.'
- 'They were there for me when things were tough and I owe it to them to stand by them.'
- 'They are the only one who understands what I'm going through.'

All the while you start alienating your own Great8™, start to isolate yourself from your great personal support, and start heading into breakdown. That causes you to get out of balance and get sucked into the Cloaked Investor's world. Your happiness will diminish, your drama and burdens will increase, your focus will be on surviving. You will resent your Cloaked Investor™ and start to blame them for your problems and, most importantly, you won't know how to get out of the relationship because you now think you need them. You can't remember your life before them and you've got very little power or confidence to stand on your own two feet. What's even harder is that you might have married them or gone into business with them or you have created a life with them that's hard to get out of or change. Boy, I know this. It happened to me a couple of times.

How to get out of this relationship:

- Own the fact that YOU are responsible for letting it grow and get out of hand.
- Put this Investor into the category of Catalyst immediately. This relationship and this person are now your rocket ship to enlightenment.
- You're going to take this relationship and all the lessons and gifts it's got for you and learn and grow from it FAST.
- Stop blaming the person and resenting the situation you are in. If they've taken all your money, remember, you gave it to them. If you have a loveless or abusive marriage, remember, you let that happen. You are the person responsible for this mess. You brought them into your Great8™.
- This situation is all about re-establishing your boundaries, expectations and communication tools to live your life according to your values. Somewhere along the line, you sold yourself out, YOU did that, nobody made you, and this person is here to be the Catalyst for you to sort yourself out and get you to re-establish your true north.
- Get direction and support from professionals who can give you strategies, and legal and financial advice. Before you change this relationship, get all the facts and really understand your position. Too many people get scared, over-react and create more drama and mess. You want to have a plan to move this person back from your inner circle of support, because they are not supporting you.

Your life won't move forward until you do this.

What's exciting is that this is a magnificent opportunity for you both to get clear about your values and directions as there is a possibility that the two of you can still have a rewarding and enriching relationship with each other. However, you MUST stop the dysfunction immediately.

Have the courage to declare the relationship unhealthy and stop it. Don't wait for them to do it; most of the time they can't or won't.

Get connected to your Anchor immediately. You need their strength, their steadfast confidence. You also need to talk to your Grounder. Get clear on the reality—finances, children, property, business, agreements etc. Get real about the facts and what it's going to take to disconnect from this person and how to manage the boundaries of the relationship.

Notice which other Great8™ investors are missing in your wheel. Create a plan of who you can bring back in. Start talking to them again and get yourself back into balance as fast as you can. You want to move forward, so don't dwell on the Cloaked Investor™ and everything they did or didn't do for you. All conversations from this point are about moving forward.

See if the Cloaked Investor™ has any real relationships outside of yours. Most of the time, they have lied to you or are in denial about a lot of things. They are not dealing in reality and you need to reset your boundaries and how much time you spend with them.

Now, if you've married them or share a business with them, the first thing you must do is support them in getting support. Professional people are ready to assist you: counsellors, psychologists, family associations, couples therapy and even life and great business coaches. I've coached people in business to sever relationships if they really weren't right.

Seek legal advice about your position and any agreements you may have. Also, lock down your finances. Start to see the reality about this person. They are not taking responsibility for themselves and YOU are enabling them. I know this is not a good thing to read, or even think about. However, if this is happening to you right now, it's the best thing for you to read and accept me as your Catalyst when I say *warning, warning, warning. You have a Cloaked Investor™ in your life and you are destined for drama and even more problems in your life if you don't do something about it NOW!*

If the Cloaked Investor™ doesn't want any support, stand back and leave them alone. Don't try to fix them. This is actually all about you anyway. Your role is not to fix anyone else. Your responsibility is to sort your life out and maybe, through example, your Cloaked Investor™ may start sorting their life out too. Maybe not. Give them a copy of this book and invite them work on their own Greatness Wheel, or suggest they come to one of my seminars or coaching programs.

8. Growth: fill your wheel, then double it, then move on

When your Greatness Wheel is full with each role filled with one person, do it again and add another person to the role. This is the backup plan for your Greatness. As you know, people will move in and out of your life, and when they do, you want to make sure you have someone else (like an understudy) that you've occasionally talked to in that role capacity that hasn't been the main Great8™ Investor. This is especially useful when one of your Great8™ is dying or very sick with a long recovery period. You can work with your Great8™ understudy and still get support and also be of support to the person who is dying or sick in whatever capacity you can.

The Greatness Principle® is all about balance and that's the goal. No matter what happens with you or others in your world, you want to support people to achieve balance. When balance is in, people think better, make better decisions, and they are more able to create results in their life and generally life just works better.

Chapter 7

When you've got your Domain wheel full and doubled up, pick another Domain and start working on that. An analogy I used with one of my clients the other day is like a magician or circus performer who's spinning lots of plates on long sticks. You want to get the first Domain spinning, before you try spinning another one.

How do you know that your Great8™ have your back?

This is a very important question. We've just talked about the Cloaked Investor™ and seen how they get into our world. Just so you know, Cloaked Investor™, by definition, isn't a bad person. They are just lost lone wolves wanting to stop the survival mode and pain of their life and are people who are not taking responsibility for themselves, their actions or their life. I know this, because I've coached many business owners who had a business partner/co-owner who was a Cloaked Investor™ and, on a personal level, I married one! Yes, my husband, Simon, from the outset, looked, acted and sounded together, he had great support, yet after we got married and had our daughter, the truth actually came out that he really didn't have support. So when I became a new mother, I had effectively stopped 'over-supporting' him. Simon's behaviour and attitude to me and our marriage became angry, dismissive and self-obsessed. He was not being his best self for about two years. Please know that I was safe and so was the baby. I was not stupid; however, I was dealing with a husband who was being a pre-schooler and having regular, ongoing tantrums and inappropriate behaviour, and that by itself wore me down.

Hindsight is a wonderful thing, and upon reflection, almost three years later, and applying the Greatness Principle®, pre-baby I had been over-supporting him in three Great8™ roles. Post-baby, I had one Great8™ role. His reaction to that lack of support in his life was not handled well. He loved our baby but also resented the change the baby had caused for him. He didn't have me and sometimes he would say, 'where has my wife gone?' He had married a woman prepared to over-support him. Now she wasn't doing that anymore. In fact, due to his behaviour and verbal abuse, I withdrew completely from supporting him to the point that we separated and lived apart for a few months. Our relationship had degraded so much that I had to let him know that the impact of who he was being was damaging, even killing, my vision and self-confidence, and compromising my character to the point of non-recognition. I loved him, but I could not be with him. I wanted to separate and STAY married. He needed to pull his act together, generate income, stop being so angry, dismissive and self-obsessed, and work together with me. When he did that, I would have him back.

It was the toughest thing I've ever had to do in my life. Also, during this time, I was still formulating the Greatness Principle® dynamics; my head and heart were in baby land; and most importantly, my own Greatness Wheel was under massive change as my old support structure was not strong. I was in a new city, my mum had died, I was now a mother, and my husband had stopped supporting me emotionally. Both our Greatness Wheels were low or on empty. We were trying to rely on each other and support each other at the same time. The main external support Simon used was alcohol. The main external support I used was food and comfort eating. Sound familiar?

Using the Greatness Principle® and also the Great8™ I have in my life in the Domains of business, marriage and motherhood, I now have over 24 people actively supporting me in my life, and Simon is only ONE of them. I also used the Greatness Principle® on him (he didn't know it at the time), and his life has completely changed. His career is now flourishing and he's achieving the best results he's ever had. So his career Domain Great8™ is full! I've reset my boundaries and I hold them firm. He's now working on other important Domains of life and success. I am one of his Great8™ and, to be honest, he still struggles with this. However, he would tell you himself that he's a better man for it as he is now responsible for the results in his life and he's totally up for the challenge of being the man he's always wanted to be. How does it get any better than that?

This doesn't happen just in personal relationships, this happens all the time in business. When I talk to a business owner and they are telling me their business challenge, it's almost certain there will be an addiction of some kind going on where they feel they need additional support: overworking (80–100 hours week), alcohol, food, an affair, online chat and relationships, drug addiction, excessive shopping, internet/social media addiction, health and fitness addiction. You'll find it where people are overdoing something and they are not balanced. When they do this, they are using this activity to try to keep balance, to soothe their emotions, still their mind, make them feel good/better or help their body process what's going on, or all of the above. Not good. People who keep doing addictive behaviour like this will then have much bigger, longer term problems. The goal is BALANCE.

So back to how do you know that your Great8™ Investors have your back. Well, initially, you don't. When you meet someone new, you need to have your eyes, ears, heart and intuition open. Solid, strong relationships develop over a long period of time. So when you are selecting people to support you, test them out. Look and listen to people you interact with. Do you like them? Do you like what they say? Do you like what they do? What do they do when under pressure? Does that inspire you? Do you appreciate them and do they honour and appreciate YOU? Do they value long-term relationships? Do they know how to have long-term relationships? Can they share any stories about how they supported someone else? Are they interested in you? Do they ask interesting questions about you? Do they listen? Do they offer support with no expectation in return? Are they consistent with you in their behaviour, words and action?

Consistency is the critical factor. For example, if you want an Enthusiast in your Greatness Wheel, the potential candidates for you will be people who are excited and positive. They are never negative or gossipy with you. They only look for and see the rainbow. They make you feel good, they are interested in you, every time they meet up with you. They ask about your projects, your work, family or the Domain you are looking to fill.

When you have found a potential Great8™ Investor, don't stop looking. Work with this one and build and test the relationship. Time will tell you if they are the right fit. Your ultimate goal is to double your wheel anyway, so keep looking to find the right fit for YOU.

If the Great8™ Investor somehow changes their support of you or isn't being themselves with you, like Simon did with me, don't discard them immediately. If you believe that they have changed unexpectedly and they are not being themselves, take a look at what is going on with their world and life. Something might be going on that is having a big impact on them and that's changing their behaviour and support to you. What's going on for them will affect you and their ability to support you. Your responsibility is to see it, understand it, and then get support, and for you to bring in one of your backups or find a new Great8™ Investor to fill that role for you.

What I love about the Greatness Principle® is that it names the game! We've got an empowering context to look at what is going on, own it and make choices about moving forward. We no longer have to blame people, situations and circumstances, spiral blindly into failure and isolate ourselves and become lone wolves. We can get up into the helicopter above our current circumstances and start to see what's going on with ourselves and other people. We can also start to appreciate our own and others' humanity and get the right advice and support to improve and grow TOGETHER.

Chapter 7

You have a choice in every moment.
Choose greatness, even if it's harder.
~ Jen Harwood

Chapter 8

The great breakdown

There is a breakdown rule. It states: if someone has four or fewer of the Great8™ in their wheel, they will soon experience or actually be experiencing breakdown, either physically, emotionally, mentally, spiritually or financially. I've seen it too many times now with a variety of clients from varied backgrounds, experiences and unique combinations of circumstances. Anyone who has four or fewer of their Great8™ active and engaged with them, from my own observation, are more likely to experience challenges in their life or the Domain they are working in. Such challenges could be, for example:

Physical—heart attack, stroke, ulcers, digestive disorders, being grossly overweight or anorexic

Financial—massive debt, serious overspending, bankruptcy

Mental—depression, social isolation, withdrawal from family/community

Emotional—anxiety, mood disorders, rage outbursts, stress-related conditions

Chapter 8

Spiritual—suicide, addictions: alcohol, drugs, sex addictions, crime. With spiritual challenges, a person's character sinks lower than ever before and they get lost as to who they are and what their purpose is.

If you think this sounds pretty depressing, I agree with you. However, from the work I have been doing and the results I've been seeing, people don't necessarily experience all of the above, or to the same extreme as others. Why bankrupt your life (or credibility) because you've been dealt a life/leadership challenge that you can't solve or deal with all on your own? Why create so much drama, destruction and social isolation because you are embarrassed, ashamed, guilty, ignorant, upset and all the other feelings and states we work ourselves up to? It's not worth it. All you've got to do is put your hand up and ask for support … listen … and consider what your Great8™ suggest, and take action.

I also acknowledge that people are going to get sick, be overly emotional, be mentally challenged and experience financial challenges and experience their character and moral compass getting off track, and that is a part of life. Just by having your Great8™ in place doesn't immunise you or anyone from drama, challenge and change. Life is happening and our goal is to embrace it and get the best support we can to deal with it, learn from it and, where possible, overcome it.

Looking back at my mother's life, Cath had a full Greatness Wheel for most of her life and especially at times of breakdown. Cath had all of her Great8™ in multiple Domains—motherhood, marriage, community, and career. She was very well connected, she had people who were investing in her, and she was listening and taking action. So you could say, technically, that the Greatness Principle® failed her. She shouldn't have got sick then with all that support, love and connection. Maybe that's right.

Looking at a bigger picture though for just a moment, maybe the reason Cath lived for almost seven years after her initial cancer diagnosis (a great deal longer than the six months that were predicted) was because she had her Great8™ Investors in place and used the support she needed to live, fight her cancer, and see all that she wanted to see and experience before she died. Getting cancer at 58 years old changed her whole life and her entire wheel of support. Cancer ended and changed the Domains she had built such as her career: she couldn't work due to chemo treatments, chemo reactions and complicated side effects making her very, very sick. It changed her physical ability to be able to be a wife in the same way (homemaker, lover, holiday companion). Cath had become 'disabled' compared to the previous cancer-free Cath. At many points over those seven years, she could hardly walk or eat or breathe. Cath's only Domain of focus was cancer.

Cath's wheel is shown below and what you'll see in that wheel is that her Catalyst was CANCER. She had a very direct relationship with cancer and it was ALIVE.

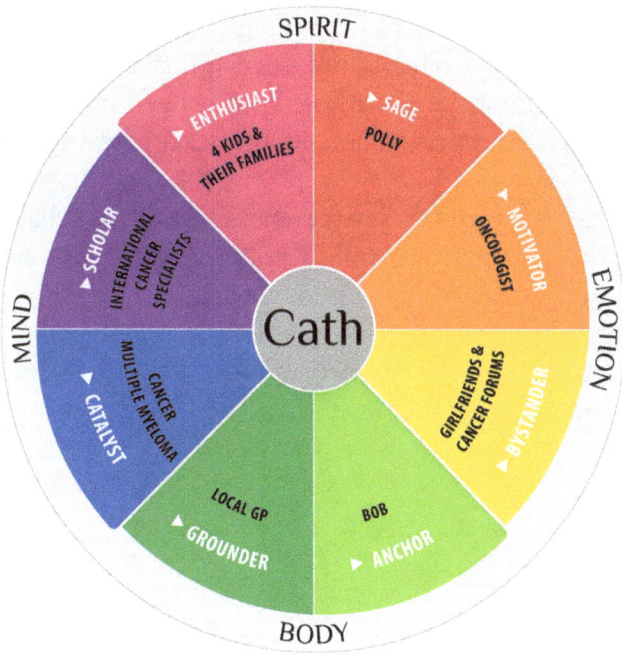

In my observation, it will start to become obvious when you are dealing with breakdown and are experiencing life or leadership bankruptcy, as you will be getting sick or losing the plot emotionally or having mental breakdowns, or you have an addiction, or are socially isolated, or all of the above. Regardless of the cause, you need to review your vision and commitment, then review your Greatness Wheel and see if you have recently lost anyone from it or if any of the roles are vacant.

Life has its ultimate turns and twists. It's an adventure, and the only thing we can count on in life is CHANGE. Change has an impact that you can immediately see and, sometimes, it is so subtle that, over time, it has a huge effect. ALL of my clients in the past 15 years experienced situations and events that changed their lives and the people in them. This in turn affected their relationships, connections and support structures. When change occurs, people's support changes and the balance that was in place will go out of balance. That's the way life works and it is best to accept that that is the way it is and work with it. There is no point dwelling on the loss, being in a tantrum about the change and that it shouldn't have happened or being fearful of the uncertainty of the future. Your life is now different. Deal with it. Face it head on, don't distract yourself. Get the support you need and start growing!

I have outlined below the top seven events/situations/life challenges that will affect the Greatness Principle® Greatness Wheel, and suggestions on how to work through them. Please note that the breakdown list is in no particular order, hierarchy of significance or even comprehensive. There are lots of things that cause breakdown of the Greatness Wheel. These are the top seven that my clients and I have faced.

Breakdown cause	Strategies to deal with the breakdown
Death or terminal illness	You've lost the person. Okay. Identify their role and look for new people to fill that role.
	Grief counselling is very helpful and a Scholar can support you on how to move through this.
	Ask one of your other Great8™ to fill in for that role while you come to terms with the loss and fill it.
	If the death isn't sudden, talk to the person who is dying and ask them to suggest a replacement. This might sound weird, however they know they are going and would love to see you still supported.
	Look at the dying person's family and friends and see who will be affected most by the loss. Be a Great8™ for them for as long as they need it.
Divorce and family separation	The couple probably shared Great8™ Investors. Pulling the relationship or family apart will automatically have both people with less than eight Investors. As the couple is going through property settlement, child custody and the like, they should also consider each person's Greatness Wheel and plan individually who they are going to have support them.
	Mutual friends don't have to be cut down the middle. Make sure the friend can still be supportive to both without feeling compromised. Make sure the friend is not the Anchor for both of you—that won't work!
	Review wheels for any children involved. When families break apart, children's lives and support structures are drastically changed. Be mindful of that change and support the child to connect with new Great8™ Investors. A child is never too young to have their parents review who the child has in their Greatness Wheel to support them be the greatest kid possible!

Breakdown cause	Strategies to deal with the breakdown
Marriage or new long-term relationship	Two separate individuals come together with their own support structure and rarely do each like and appreciate every one of the other's Great8™ Investors. It is predictable that each one will consider the other's needs higher than their own in the honeymoon period, and will cut off or disengage from some of their Great8™ to please their new partner.
	The couple needs to get clear about the relationship they want to create and WHO they want to be in it. When they know who they want to be, they can then each consider and build their own Greatness Wheel to support that.
	The couple needs clear boundaries around the Domains each are supporting the other in. Just because the husband is in business doesn't mean the wife is an automatic and willing supporter. You both get to choose and HOLD the boundary.
New baby, first time parents in particular, surprise babies	When a baby comes into a relationship, roles and responsibilities change. Typically, the prime carer is focussed on the child and the other parent is usually working hard to pay for it all! The prime carer's whole world has changed and they are now no longer working, studying or doing their 'old thing' and are at home with the baby, usually quite isolated mentally and emotionally. It is vital for the prime carer to build a support network to be a great parent.
	On the flip side, the parent who is out working hard no longer has the same level of support from their partner, as the partner is focussed on the baby. The working parent must replace the role with an appropriate support structure for 3–12 months until the prime carer comes out of baby land.
	The baby/child needs their own Greatness Wheel considered. If the child is with a single parent, then that parent needs to create a support structure for themselves and their child. It's easy to get into being a martyr and doing everything for the child and not for you. That's actually over-supporting! This is harsh to hear and if someone had said that to me when my baby was little, I would have been completely offended. So if that's you ... breathe. Your child needs you, your partner, siblings and grandparents and if you don't have those to offer, you need to look further. Look for playmates and childcare facilities to give you a break and for your child to interact and learn from other kids. If you want your child to be great, you need to let go and build and nurture their Great8™.

The great breakdown

Breakdown cause	Strategies to deal with the breakdown
Job change: new job, lost job, retirement	**New Job:** be open to the people in your new company. Be yourself and be open to 'making friends'. Listen more than you speak so that you can identify what type of people you are working with. If this job is a new challenge and stretches you, make sure you have support from your external Great8™ so you can keep doubts, concerns and worries outside of work. **Lost Job:** being made redundant or fired isn't usually a pleasant experience. Many people feel a sense of shame, guilt or embarrassment. Talk about it with your Great8™. Be supported in this process so you can recover quickly and choose a new adventure. **Retirement:** this is an interesting time for people. Their working career has been a huge focus and now it's not there anymore. Many people have their whole Great8™ Wheel from people they work with. So retirement can be incredibly lonely as the person feels lost and alone. The retiree needs to create a new vision for this next chapter of their life. Direct them to think about what they've always wanted to do and haven't had time for because they were working. Create a vision around that and start finding Great8™ Investors to support them with their new vision.
Moving, relocation	As our Greatness Wheel is usually filled with people we see in person, when we move to a new town, city, state or country, we are no longer in contact with them the same way. Make sure you keep in regular contact with your long distance Great8™ when you move to the new place. Through phone calls, emails and skype sessions, they can support you to transition into the new location and take the pressure off having to identify new potential people to fill your Greatness Wheel quickly. Some of our Great8™ are with us for life, no matter where we live, so if you have one of them, stay in regular contact and organise to see each other in person yearly. Take your time to 'adopt' new people into your Greatness Wheel. You've moved into a whole new world and this new community has a different style, energy and identity to the old place. Listen, watch and learn how this new group works. Once you've done that, then you can go deeper. Also, if anyone asks you to join their group, go along and visit. Keep testing, checking and watching until you feel you've got a strong connection with a person or group.

Breakdown cause	Strategies to deal with the breakdown
Financial change: bankruptcy or windfall	Money changes everything, whether you have lots of it or lose all of it. When you have a lot of money or get a lot fast through various means, people want to be with you and some of your friends will stop wanting to be with you. Your Greatness Wheel of support will change and you will have vacancies in the wheel. It comes down to TRUST. Be mindful about the people approaching you and check to see that they have your best interests at heart. Are they wanting to be part of your life because of YOU or your money?
	When you lose all your money and/or go bankrupt, many people feel a huge amount of shame, guilt and despair. They try to cover it up, they withdraw back into their homes and privacy and try just to survive it. The problem with this is that they make failing and bankruptcy mean something so significant that they can't see anything else. They then kill off support and relationships to cover it up. That doesn't work and makes the matter WORSE.
	Money is not WHO you are. If you've lost it or got it, create the vision (picture) you want to achieve in your life and start being disciplined to do the actions you need to do every day to make it happen.

When you or someone you know experiences one of these challenges, it's time to sit down and look at how that challenge is going to affect the Greatness Wheel dynamic. If you are doing this for yourself, you can start to identify who is missing and possible candidates whom you can approach to spend time with. If you have lots of people offering themselves to you to support you, graciously acknowledge the offers and then, as objectively as you can, choose who would be the best person in each role to help you fulfil your vision. Be strategic; be committed to your vision. Refrain from being flattered by the offers of support. You want the best people in your team to support your Greatness in the Domain of life that is important to you. Choose wisely.

If you are reviewing a Greatness Wheel for someone who's currently experiencing any of the challenges listed above, start to identify their Great8™ gaps and work out which role they need. Then work out which role suits you best and start to interact with them in that context. This is a very empowering strategy for you and your subject as you don't need to be everything they need or 'rescue' them from their challenge. You can support them with a clear role and committed relationship that works for both of you.

For example, John, a farmer in Central Victoria, Australia, whom I met through a speaking event, was having a major challenge as his wheat farm had been affected by drought for eight years. The silos on the property only had in them the last batch of seed that he owned. He didn't have any more money to buy more seed as his credit with the banks had been extended as far as it could go. John was a business man, his property was very big and he had a team of men who worked for him. He had been smart in the more bountiful years to diversify his services and bought specific equipment to create a part-time landscaping business with his team to keep the guys in work and also to keep cash flow coming in.

I went inside John's modest farmhouse and his wife, Ruth, offered me a cup of tea and a slice of homemade cake. She was happy I was there as something had to be done. They had three children, the youngest of whom was 14. Ruth had heard John speak about seeing me on stage at a business event and said that John had thought at the time that I was the person to make it happen for them.

John and Ruth told me their story. Their agribusiness consultant was sitting there with us as well (one of the team for the company whose annual conference I had spoken at). John and Ruth were on the brink of losing everything and I realised that who I was going to be for John and his wife was critical to their moving forward. John had great support from Ruth (Anchor), his workers (Enthusiasts), the local bank manager (Grounder), his father who lived on the property as well (Sage), all the other local farmers (Bystanders), and the local agribusiness consultant sitting next to me (Scholar). After talking more and digging around in conversation I realised that John's Catalyst was the local chamber of commerce president who was encouraging him to develop the landscaping business. This farmer and his wife wanted

Chapter 8

me to help them thrive. Knowing the Greatness Principle®, I knew what to do. It was obvious to me that my job was to be his Motivator and get him into action. Sitting around and hoping it wouldn't rain too much to wash away the topsoil, that it would be sunny enough for the seed to grow and flourish and that the weather wouldn't flatten the crop before it was ready to harvest couldn't be the strategy to rely on.

The mission was to turn around the farm and the business so they had a steady source of income all year round, regardless of the weather, AND to get out of debt. So, as great Motivators do, I supported them in creating a plan of action to work on all elements of the business, the farm, the relationship between Ruth and John, their staff and their actions, behaviours and activities, as well as their involvement in the community. I whipped John's head into gear to secure his vision and goal about what he wanted to achieve so that it was unmessable. Unmessable means that no-one's opinions, comments or actions were going to crush, destroy or affect his vision and his commitment to it.

John was on a mission to MAKE IT HAPPEN. No hype, no rah rah and fanfare, just head down and DO IT. John was so focussed that when he shared with his Great8™ Investors the vision of what he was doing, they all offered even more support. The bank manager was a bit more flexible and offered a bit more finance for equipment, the accountant offered to do some forecasting and financial modelling at no extra charge, the workers all told their friends and family about the landscaping options, which generated leads, and it was great. John and Ruth got through the drought, that last crop grew and was harvested, which paid off a lot of the pressing debt, and they replanted for the next year. John's son now runs the landscaping business full time.

The reason why John had a great outcome was that he was prepared to be vulnerable and TRUST everyone in his Great8™. Even me, a 36-year-old single, childless woman who didn't know the first thing about farming but who knew a lot about getting people to create visions, causing them to focus and getting them into action to achieve them.

John is the hero, not me, not any of his Great8™, because he shared, he was honest, and he listened and accepted the advice, strategies and corrective feedback he received.

John had this GREAT success because he made the result more important than his own ego and emotions. I always say to people, 'do you want to stay trapped in this circumstance, or do you want the vision? Choose!' If they are not prepared to tell anyone what's going on, because they are ashamed, guilty, embarrassed, afraid, worried or concerned about being judged, I tell them that they have not had enough pain yet, walk away and wait for them to come and ask for support.

It's their mess, not mine, and I am more than willing to support them WHEN THEY ASK FOR IT. I learned a long time ago that rescuing doesn't work. They don't learn anything if they are continually being saved. In fact, what they do learn from being rescued and 'helped' is that when they get into the next challenge, they can expect to be rescued by you! That is not good for them, and is exhausting and draining for you.

How to rebuild your Greatness Wheel

Having vacancies and gaps in your Greatness Wheel is actually a good thing. This allows you to go and actively choose people to involve in your life and you're actually choosing on purpose. Here are some strategies and things to consider when rebuilding or creating Greatness.

1. Stop and breathe. It can't get any worse now that you know what's going on. The lights are on in a Domain that was in darkness and you were stumbling around bumping into stuff and getting lost. You now know where you are, what you are doing and that you don't have any support in this area and/or you are being 'over-supported' by someone. Knowledge is power!

2. Focus on the future, not the present. Like the first point, creating a new vision for your life is essential to move you. You've got to have something to move towards to give you energy.

3. You are not your circumstances. You are not a bank balance, failed business, bankrupt, test result, diagnosis, injury, disability, mental condition, vagrant, victim, loser or any of the things that your current circumstances suggest. This is just the reality of where you are right now. It doesn't have to be who or what you are for the rest of your life! Stop playing the mental records of what's going on: it creates nothing.

4. Review and develop your skills and personal awareness. Do you need some training in communication, listening, anger management, dealing with an addiction (alcohol, drugs, sex, violence)? Do you need to learn a new profession or trade? Does your health or body need attention? Do you need to rest more, exercise more, eat less or get medical support? Put a plan in place and tell your Motivator!

5. Get real. Acknowledge that the current situation isn't working anymore. Acceptance is the hardest part of this. You've created a mess of your Domain and YOU have to clean it up. Your mummy isn't coming along to sort out your life, clean your room or do it for you. You're a grown up. It's time to take responsibility for what's working and, most importantly, what's not working.

6. Look at who is still with you and acknowledge their love for you. It doesn't matter what your circumstances, there will be at least one person in your life who is still with you. They may have been the dumping ground for all of your complaints, whinging and blaming. You may have treated them badly, dismissed them, been rude and nasty to them and even done everything you could to get rid of them. Guess what? They are still there, and they are still supporting YOU. They love you, and it's time you start being grateful for their investment of time, energy, money and love in you and thank them for their support.

7. Identify your major Domains e.g. work, marriage, parenting, health, sport, family. In my experience, everyone has three main Domains in life that are really important to them. Figure out which are your top three and understand the reason why they are your top three.

8. Pick a Domain that is critical and not working right now, and create a new vision for it. Get out the paper, coloured pencils, magazines, and scissors and glue, and create a picture of the dream and vision of your future in that Domain. Focus on the details. The more specific, the better. You can create this vision board by searching for pictures on your favourite search engine or by using online vision board tools. Just do it, print it out and put it somewhere prominent and where you can look at it A LOT and often!

9. Brainstorm potential people and write their names in the roles. Don't choose anyone yet, just think about all the people you know, or would like to know to support you with your new vision, and write them all down.

10. Pick the role that you think you need first. Look at the list of people you have chosen who could fit that role. Now pick one and make contact with that person. Send an email, pick up the phone, go visit, attend a seminar. Go out into the world and start to connect. You don't need to announce that you want them to be your Great8™ Investor—that would probably freak them out. Just be with them. Listen to them, listen to who they are being, their vision for their life/domain, their personal awareness, and listen to their character.

11. Invest in someone else. Sometimes it's hard to even contemplate acknowledging our own weakness or dire circumstances for a variety of reasons. I get it. One strategy that can really work is when you focus on someone else. Lone wolves are usually focussed on themselves. To break the habit and open yourself up

Chapter 8

a bit, go and be the Investor you need in your wheel for someone else. Make them your secret project, and as they start being great, you'll find that you can relate to others and you will get both a benefit and return from investing in someone else.

12. Join a new group. Sometimes we need to get out and about to attend events, community activities and social groups to find our Great8™ Investors. As much as it is easier and more comfortable to stay at home, we need to get out and about and BE OPEN to finding people whom we connect with and like.

13. Choose your investors S L O W L Y. You want the right support to fulfil your vision. This isn't a tick-the-box-and-move-on exercise. You are going to share yourself with these people; you want to be able to trust them. You want to be able to trust their advice, their perspective and their experience. You want to make sure they have your best interests at heart. So take your time until you are sure, then go for it.

14. Ask your other Great8™ to support you, or meet a prospective candidate. Yes, I sound like I'm a recruitment agent for a company. Well, it's a bit similar. You've got a vacant role, you want to fill it. You need to look at potential people, check them out and then do reference checks and background checks. Your other Great8™ will tell you if a potential person fits. I'll never forget my accountant Cara Hall (Grounder) saying to me one day, 'Jen, I've seen this sort of thing before. That guy will move into your business, spend all the money, make you think it's your fault and then expect you to work hard while he lives off your generosity for the rest of your life. He's not right for your business and he's not right for you.' All I can say is that Cara was right and, lucky for me, I followed her advice. When your Great8™ tell you things like this, LISTEN and take immediate action.

15. Spend time with the Great8™ Investors you need. Meet them for coffee, do their training event, go on a weekend away, read their

books. DO whatever to be with them and absorb their wisdom, advice, strategies and everything they have to offer you.

16. Shut up and listen. Your Great8™ are going to give you Corrective Feedback about your challenges and situation, and how you can move forward towards your great vision. LISTEN to them. No buts, no interruptions, be quiet, be grateful, say thank you and then take action.

17. TAKE MASSIVE ACTION! Sitting around doing nothing won't create anything. DO THE WORK, step by step and greatness will flood towards you.

18. Share with your Great8™ Investors how well you are doing. They are your life ring of support, and totally invested in YOU. Share with them your results, tell them the great stories and adventures you are having. Share the successes and little wins and be open and honest and transparent with them. Unlike most people you will meet, your Great8™ really want to know and will sit and listen for as long as you want!

What if you have a full wheel and the Great8™ you have aren't good?

This happens a lot. When people become aware of the Greatness Principle®, they may have their wheel full or almost full and yet are not experiencing greatness in the Domain they are examining. Now don't go dumping all the people you think are no good or are not supporting you. Remember, these people have all invested in you and care about you. That's still a very valuable asset. What you do in this situation is make sure you are clear about your vision, then go and re-share it with them and ASK them to contribute to it. Most of the time, we haven't engaged our Great8™ Investors and we are just expecting them to help. Isn't that just silly! This is your vision, your goal, your future. The person who wants this the most is YOU. You need to go back to the people you already have and touch, move and inspire them about your vision for this Domain and how they can support you achieve that.

For example, Steve was a consultant who came to see me on the recommendation of a friend. Steve had been out of work for six months, due to a company restructure that resulted in his contract to be terminated. He was the co-carer for his four children aged 8 to 16 with his ex-wife. He had good cushion of money left from the settlement of the divorce, so he was very comfortable. He'd been on his own for a very long time and only 6 months prior had found a girlfriend who loved him and his children. She was actually over-supporting him and he relied on her to tell him what to do with the children, and how to manage the ex-wife. She'd come make dinner for the family and also try to coach him on his business as he wasn't getting any new contracts. Steve is a lovely man and he just wasn't getting his act together to take charge of his life and be the leader he'd been in the past.

I met with Steve and listened to his story. I did the Greatness Principle® Greatness Wheel with him and it was clear that he had lots of support. He even had a business coach (Motivator). I was really curious why he needed to talk to me. He already had a Motivator ... After listening a bit more, I realised that Steve wasn't demanding results in his life. He was talking and complaining to everyone who would listen, yet there was no action.

The best strategy for Steve was to go back to his Motivator and his other Great8™ Investors, take responsibility for his current results and be a NEW demand for Greatness with them. He had to be committed to wanting the vision (which was to have solid contracts and income, marry his girlfriend and be a great example for his kids) more than anything.

Wishing for something and being driven or compelled to have it are two different things. Sometimes you have to get into a place where you are either moving to get away from something so bad you don't want any more (PAIN) or moving towards a vision that's so awesome, brilliant and the best possibility you can dream of (PLEASURE). Use whichever is going to move you forward and don't stop, or give up or be distracted until you get there.

Chapter 8

You're in the midst of a war, a battle between the limits of a crowd seeking the surrender of your dreams, and the power of your true vision to create and contribute. It is a fight between those who will tell you what you cannot do, and that part of you that knows, and has always known, that we are more than our environment, and that a dream, backed by an unrelenting will to attain it, is truly a reality with an imminent arrival.
~ Tony Robbins

Chapter 9

Wheel dynamics

Having worked with so many people, I've noticed a few patterns when people have some of their Great8™ people missing. You will probably relate to one of these, or know someone who's in this pattern. They are people with only five of the Great8™ Investors. As you've already learned so far, when you have five or more of the Great8™ in place, life will work. You can achieve results and there is less drama in your life. There is, however, an opportunity to be greater than you already are. So let's have a look at the four most common patterns and see where you or someone you know fits.

Chapter 9

Free Spirits

Free Spirit patterns have Enthusiasts everywhere, a couple of Sages plus Bystanders, a soft Motivator and a Scholar. These people are happy, joyful, optimistic, full of ideas, and usually have no money and no assets. They don't worry about their security or being wealthy or rich. They don't want to be confined by day-to-day details. They seem to have the universe provide for them, which usually ends up being an over-generous family member, friend, church group or 'community'. These people want to 'heal the world', bring peace to all and live in harmony.

They are fun to be with, and many have no sense of time, responsibility, consequences or commitment. They are 'in the zone' or 'at one with the universe'. The types of businesses/professions they typically go into are the spiritual, healing and etheric domains. They might be healers, artists, creatives or musicians.

Now before you start throwing rocks at me, there is nothing wrong with these people, their professions or business styles. What I have noticed is that they don't have the Anchor, Grounder or Catalyst in their Greatness Wheel. To be great in their spiritual domain they need to get clarity, accountability, reality and a kick in the right direction! Let's face it, the best healer or masseuse isn't going to have a great business/career if they can't charge for their services, manage money, rebook clients, manage their own cash flow or fund their own retirement.

Greatness strategy for Free Spirits:

1. Create the vision of what you really want to achieve and commit to doing whatever it takes to make it happen. Realise that you are going to feel uncomfortable and challenged, and that it's going to be hard, boring and routine—not your style. However, you are out of balance, and if you are really serious about healing the world or making a difference on this earth, you've got to get support that can contribute to your magical vision.
2. Seek out and find an Anchor, Grounder, and Catalyst! Don't stop looking until you find them. Remember, these people are not going to be easy for you to have a relationship with as they will be serious, process driven and ask lots and lots of questions. They won't accept answers like, 'God is guiding me, he will provide the way when he's ready or … I will go meditate on this or … that's limiting my awareness or creativity or … the vibes aren't good!' These types of responses will drive your Grounder mad and cause your Catalyst to ask more questions. It's time for you to get in this earthly world. Keep your joy and spirit soaring AND work with the humans on the planet to realise enlightenment for all, not just you!
3. Spend more time than you would normally feel comfortable with these three new Great8™ Investors. The reason I say this is that you don't like what they have to say or how they say it. If you want your vision to happen, then you've got to learn these elements of business and life and these three Great8™ Investors are prepared and willing to make sure that you learn and apply them.

Chapter 9

The Turbo Chargers

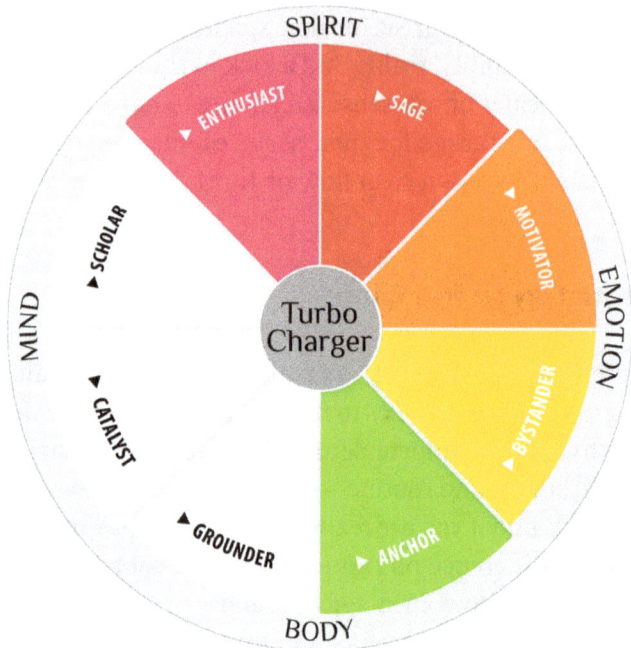

Stand back! These people are on a mission to get where they are going at record speed. Driven, focussed and pumped, these people have several Enthusiasts, a Sage, several Motivators, Bystanders, and their Anchor. They are driven by emotions and they are somewhat grounded by their Anchor. Highly emotionally driven, they channel their emotion and energy to grow, build, drive and create results.

The problem these people have is that they often don't think. They make stupid, careless choices as they don't have a Grounder, Catalyst and especially a Scholar. They are so busy turbocharging ahead that they don't think, don't plan, and they have very little time to react to problems and changes or be able to think through and take on opportunities. In business, Turbo Chargers make lots of money and also pay a higher price on things because they were distracted with a million other priorities. As they move forward, focussed only on the goal they want, many of them regularly get parking fines, speeding fines, late penalties for lodgement of forms etc. Many of my clients who are Turbo Chargers just shrug it off and say, it's the cost of getting the result, no big deal. Others would see them as wasteful and over-indulgent when in actual fact they are just moving so fast, they don't have time to think of a better way.

Greatness strategy for Turbo Chargers:

1. You've got the vision and you are in action. Your challenge is to actually slow down. What's needed here from the Catalyst role isn't the usual confronting or controversial approach. It's the calm, slow, considered 'stop and smell the daisies' approach. This will be very hard for you to accept as you know two speeds—flat out or asleep! Go find someone that you can sit still with and just be … Oooh, I can hear you shudder at that suggestion (good, it's what you need!). You've also got to take care of your body. Many Turbo Chargers run high on adrenalin and are depleted in their nutrition, which reduces your health and vitality.
2. Talk with your Grounder and create a PLAN for your life and your business. Identify what's most important to you and how much it's going to cost, how much time it needs, basically get all the facts so you've got a clear idea about what milestones you need to hit. That will ensure you can still go fast; you will just know you are headed in the right direction and will not pay such a high price for everything.
3. Find a Scholar. You've got to start talking about what you are currently doing because you really are doing it the hard way or the long way. I realise you've just got on with what needs to be done; however, you are missing innovation and ideas on how to do things more effectively and profitably with less of your effort. If you are not exhausted and overrun now, you will be, so find your Scholar and start thinking. This will prolong your life, heal your body and make you more balanced.

Chapter 9

The Plodders

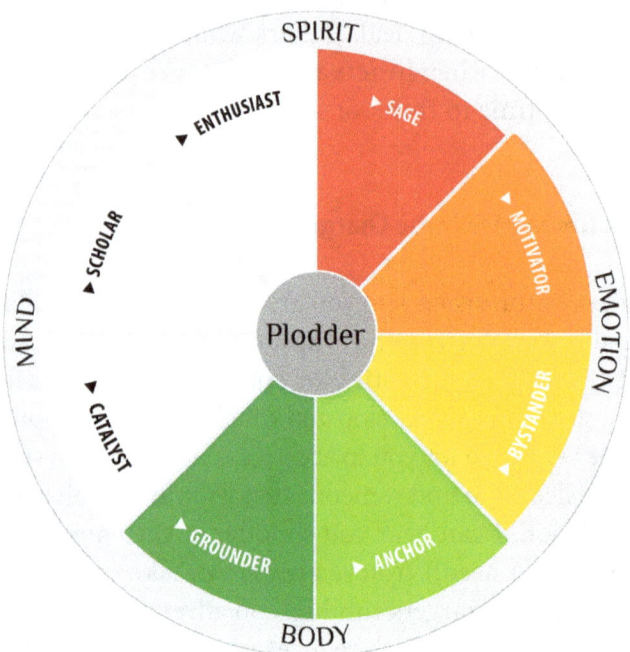

These are the 'good people' who consistently deliver results. They may not be the most impressive results, yet they deliver on time, every time. The problem is, they play the safe and secure game and have never really taken themselves out for a spin to see how Great they could really be. Some of these people secretly wish they could 'give it a go'; however, for them, safety and security trumps possibility every time.

Plodders tend to hang around in groups and do safe, sensible things. They are usually good at investing, saving and running a stable business. Typical businesses or professions that plod are accountants, consultants, manufacturers, financial planners, investment advisors. It makes sense, really, because those industries must be grounded in reality, and know who they are and what they are doing. The Plodders don't see any perceived value in shaking things up, getting overexcited or changing strategy when the current strategy is working. Does that sound like you or someone you know?

Greatness strategy for Plodders:

1. Enthusiasts can be easily dismissed by the Plodder as just a silly bunch of excitable people who deliver no tangible value. However, Enthusiasts are the best encouragers on the Greatness Wheel and they naturally manage to wiggle deep into the tiniest of ideas and encourage them to grow. They germinate possibility and, for the Plodders, when the occasional idea to be great pops into their head, they need to speak to an Enthusiast, not another Plodder, to allow the idea to grow.
2. It's time to ramp things up a bit to realise your Greatness. You need a Catalyst. That might be a business coach, a personal development program or a holiday that jolts you out of the hum drum and predictability of your life. You are doing great now, there's nothing wrong with you, and I know you could be so much more, and the way to get there is to stretch and grow your muscles of dealing with the unknown. Catalysts get you uncomfortable and when that happens … you grow and learn faster.
3. You, of course, are doing something right as your life is stable, calm and relatively drama free. Congratulations! It's hard to admit you don't know enough, especially when you are getting consistent results. On the flip side, are you leveraging your time, money and resources? Are you missing opportunities and possibilities in business, career and life? The only way to find out is to start seeking out and talking to a Scholar. An expert in areas that can leverage the Domain you are in would be a big advantage and have you be even greater, with minimal risk.

Gauntlet Runners

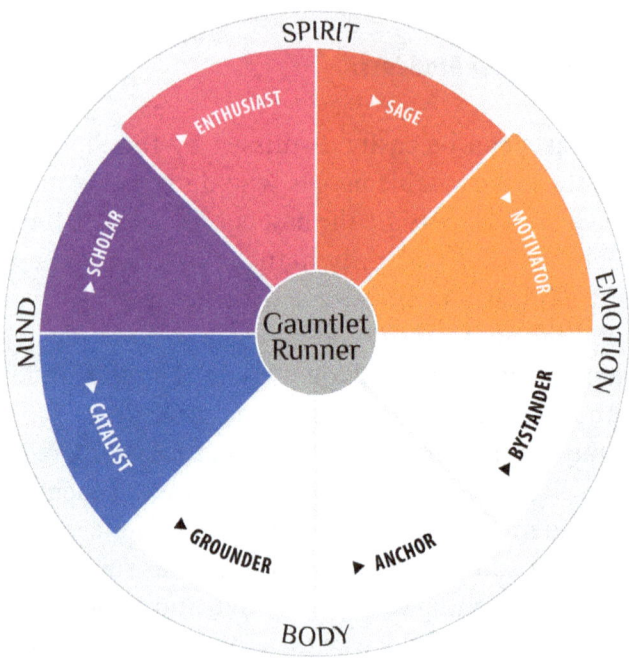

The Gauntlet Runners are emotionally switched off and digging in. Unlike the other four patterns, this person has their Catalyst in their Great8™. I've seen this one a lot in business. Something 'happens' to them (Catalyst—a situation or a person) that emotionally sets them off and they get into action with their head down, oblivious to anything else as they run hard and fast down the gauntlet for survival! They are usually fearful and uncertain, and can be deeply angry. They feel numb, disconnected and lost. They are in total survival mode and they will ignore the pain of the emotional and physical toll to themselves and will ignore the fallout of consequences to anyone else. Their prime objective is to try to understand what's happening, deal with personal vision, values and virtues challenged by the Catalytic event/person, and try to get stability and normality back as fast as possible.

These people typically make hard, fast decisions that may affect a lot of people and may hurt other people through their decisions such as divorce, business partner separation, instantly resigning from their job, selling off part of the business, firing a staff member who has made only a little mistake. The Gauntlet Runner's position in life is that they must survive and 'don't want to lose everything', so they focus on that, whatever the cost.

Given this pattern, these people are launched into massive action by the Catalyst, are armed with ideas (Scholar), have a loud cheer squad (Enthusiast), are backed up by their Sage and then get a coach (Motivator) to set the path and accountability to make it happen. Without knowing the Greatness Principle®, you'd think this combination of support would be excellent.

The problem with this pattern is that there is no-one Grounding or Anchoring them or giving them independent Corrective Feedback or support. One of the reasons the Gauntlet Runner bolts so hard into action is because they are not confident about who they are and what to do (Anchor). If they were secure in themselves, they would not doubt themselves so much and then try to overcompensate.

The other problem with this pattern is that the Catalytic event (cancer, drug addiction, crime) or person (marriage affair, family member threatening suicide, deep personal debt) is a shameful one, and the Gauntlet Runner will not talk about it to anyone. It is a secret they must bear the burden of and do the best they can to fix it, manage it or survive it.

Now, the types of Catalysts they are facing (mentioned above) generally can't be 'fixed' and dealt with alone. You need others' support to work it through and move from survive to thrive.

Chapter 9

Greatness strategy for Gauntlet Runners:

1. Pick one of your existing Great8™ Investors and tell them what's happened ASAP. Listen to their advice, suggestions and recommendations of people and experts who can support you. Follow up all recommendations.
2. Get connected to a Grounder. For some, that might be a doctor, an accountant, a support group, a psychologist, a counsellor, a specialist, or an expert, who can assess the situation and give you the reality as to what's going on, why, and the best plan of attack to deal with it.
3. STOP running so hard. You are making mistakes, and the faster you go, the more you are road kill on the highway of your life. Delegate as many jobs, tasks and responsibilities as you can for the moment so you create less 'damage' and have the time to deal with the reality you face.
4. Connect with an Anchor. That might be an individual, a group or a program to 'find yourself'. Sounds a bit airy fairy; however, you don't trust yourself right now. You've forgotten who you are. That self-distrust is making you do and say crazy things that can and will financially, emotionally, mentally and physically hurt you and others.
5. Understand that at the moment you are completely out of control and you need support. You are not bad, you are not a failure, you are not a loser. It's the complete opposite. In fact, of all people, YOU have the ability, mental strength and determination to overcome any obstacle and you need a real live Anchor, Grounder and Bystander to talk to face-to-face to balance you out.

The Drama Makers

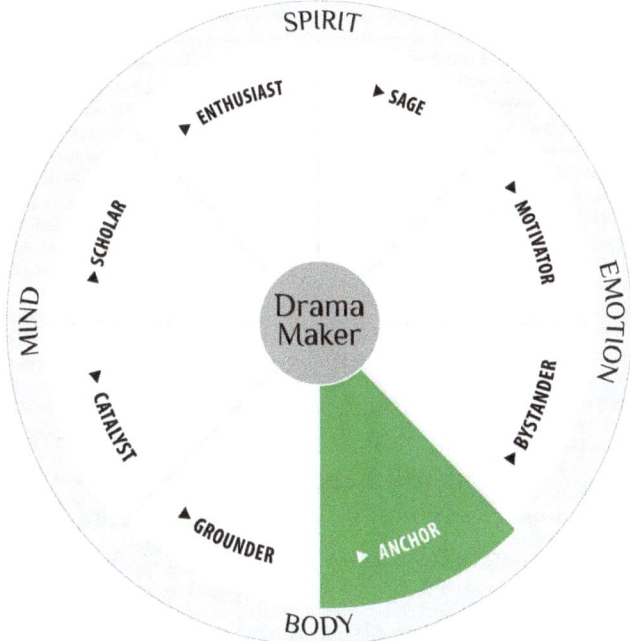

These people have the most drama in their life. They are like a shell on the beach that is washed up to shore, then dragged back into the ocean, then pummelled around in the swash and then dumped back onto shore, only to be dragged back into the sea at high tide or a big storm and have the cycle go all over again. These people are in a lot of pain. They are incredibly lonely and usually experiencing social and emotional isolation.

Dreadful things keep happening to them—they have had several businesses fail, several people in their life die close together, they lose their job, they have car accidents, their car gets broken into, they have things stolen, they are mugged or physically assaulted, they lose all their money, they are the victim of a crime or committed a crime, and sometimes they attempt or threaten to suicide. They may have had multiple divorces, they owe the tax office lots of money that

Chapter 9

they can't pay, they are in financial breakdown and physically they are not well either. I could go on, and I'm sure you know someone in your life who has been this way or is this way.

As you can see from the pattern, they have only one Great8™ Investor in place: the Anchor. The Anchor knows their true potential and, in my experience, is emotionally connected to them. It could be a family member or a spouse or someone they are in a relationship with. The Drama Maker has destroyed all the other 'good' Great8™ Investor relationships and the Anchor holds tight.

The Drama Makers aren't in survival mode, they are actually going backwards. Now, I have personally experienced someone in my life in this position and I can tell you, because of all the drama these people are in, sometimes you just want to disown them, cut them off and hope they sort themselves out, which they probably won't do. They can cost you a lot of money, drain your emotional energy, take up most or all of your mental capacity trying to solve their problems, and physically, they can run you into the ground. It is heavy going, and a lot of the time their problems are complicated and not your everyday 'normal person' issues to deal with.

Drama Makers have a Greatness Wheel that is actually full of negative supporters who don't have the Drama Maker's best interests at heart. Their wheel consists of a drug dealer or sex worker or crime cohorts, and external supports such as drugs and alcohol are in the wheel to 'help' the Drama Maker feel good about themselves and create stability and a sense of balance. What's right off track is their vision, their character, their values and virtues. To create balance, they've adopted this world of drama and negative Investors and this creates more instability and balance and they become even more addicted, and that takes them further away from Greatness.

The Drama Makers need lots of support and whomever supports a Drama Maker will need support too. I've seen it work incredibly well in a family that took their 20 year old son and did a 'family intervention' on him. They all decided who they were going to be and with professionals supporting the son and the family, they managed to change the son's Greatness Wheel and Great8™ Investors in it over a two-year period. These are the strategies the family used.

Greatness strategies for Drama Makers:

1. Professional advice was sought first from Grounders such as doctors, psychologists, case workers and other direct experts about this Drama Maker's situation. The parents made a plan of who they were going to engage first. The Drama Maker wasn't involved in this conversation.
2. Each family member agreed to be the role they were allocated. For example: the brother who normally clashed with the Drama Maker CHOSE to not clash and to just listen. He was being the Bystander. The aunt chose to be the Enthusiast and came over to visit the family more and make a point of being interested and upbeat about the Drama Maker's life, no matter how depressed, angry or rude he was. The brother and the aunt could deal with the rejection and push back because they had a bigger game they were playing.
3. The Anchor had a tough conversation with the Drama Maker and spoke to him as the little seven-year-old boy who was innocent, loving and believed the same seven-year-year old values he had lost. From that perspective, the Anchor lovingly reminded the Drama Maker that he wasn't taking responsibility for his life and the pressure/burden on the family was very heavy. The Drama Maker was open to the conversation. The Greatness Principle® was not mentioned.
4. The Anchor suggested it would be good for the Drama Maker to reconnect with one of his best mates from school with whom he hadn't talked for a while. When a Drama Maker spends time with a Bystander, they can start to see other's ways of living and other activities they might enjoy, and that they may just have fun with friends. That's the goal: to have support friendships with people who are positive and genuine. The Anchor provided a

little money and dropped him off at football so the Drama Maker could meet with his old mate. Funnily enough, the Drama Maker had an enjoyable afternoon with no drama!

5. To begin real change, the next step was to engage a Scholar: an expert to tell the Drama Maker about his options and get into his head a bit. The Drama Maker has to ultimately choose to change their life. As hard as it is for you, if they don't want to choose change, that's their choice. As the Drama Maker's experience with his old mate was so good, he was open to the Anchor suggesting the next person to connect with was a General Practitioner who specialised in teenage mental health and psychotic disorders. This was a difficult task, as every time the appointment was made, the Drama Maker suddenly couldn't make it. There were at least 15 appointments missed. Finally the Anchor got clever and organised to meet the Drama Maker for coffee three minutes' walk away from the doctor's office. Lured on false pretences, the Drama Maker protested a lot, and after a convincing talk by the Anchor WENT to the appointment. The Anchor was again playing a bigger picture. He wasn't there wanting to be liked. He wanted the result for his son. The doctor prescribed medication and referred the Drama Maker to other experts. That was what everyone was hoping for. You can't get specific medical or psychiatric support or access into specific programs without a referral.

6. It's important to note that, at this point, the Anchor was emotionally and mentally exhausted. He needed a lot of support and naturally, as the new Great8™ came into play, he didn't have to 'hold the space' the same way any more. The Anchor needed time to recover, and his Great8™ were all in on having his son's life transform. Effectively the Drama Maker had at least 24 people actively aware of the Greatness Principle Project on his life and were supporting the 'front line' people or creating circumstances or situations to support the process.

7. The next person who showed up in the Drama Maker's life was one of his best friends in primary school (Sage). They were inseparable as kids and like brothers. He had heard from the

Bystander that they'd caught up and he was wondering how the Drama Maker was, so he rang. This is what is very exciting about the Greatness Principle®: as the person starts to move towards greatness, people start to show up. The Sage hadn't been in contact with the Drama Maker for over 10 years. When he saw how messed up the Drama Maker's life was, he didn't judge him or treat him any differently. He invited him back into the old group of mates and to other activities and hobbies that the Sage was into. This lack of judgement was the breath of life that the Drama Maker needed. This old buddy related to the Drama Maker like they were still best friends as kids. The Sage (a young 20-year-old single man—Sages don't have to be old) had a wisdom, love and acceptance that touched the Drama Maker deeply. The family didn't share the Greatness Principle® Plan with the Sage at this point and they haven't ever since.

8. At this point the Drama Maker was conflicted. The Negative Investors were inviting him to do drugs, crime and other interesting activities while the Bystander and Sage mates were inviting him to play sport, hang out and have a great time. The family kept their roles strong and invited over the Bystander, Sage and others to the house to encourage more support.

9. The tide started to turn when the Drama Maker began to play one of the Bystander's sports. The coach of the Bystander's team took a special interest in the Drama Maker and offered him more games and to play at higher levels—excellent! This was great for a number of reasons: it got the Drama Maker focussed on something that wasn't drama, drugs or destructive; it made the Drama Maker feel really good and want to play more; when you play sport you have to be sober, you have to stop doing drugs as much and physical activity is a natural happy drug. The other benefit of this was that the Drama Maker now had something interesting and non-drama to talk about whereas before, he didn't talk about much as there was nothing 'good' to talk about.

10. The next Great8™ role that automatically came in was the Enthusiast. The Drama Maker was cleaning up his act, having a good time with great friends and feeling better about himself.

He was in more of a reality of his life and starting to take responsibility. All of a sudden the Drama Maker, the lone wolf was … in a relationship! Love was happening and when we are in love, enthusiasm abounds. The Drama Maker wasn't focussed anywhere near as much on himself because there was someone else to be attentive to. The relationship gave him a lot of happiness and joy. He was smiling more and he had something positive and interesting to talk about all the time.

11. The last Great8™ Investor that came in was an employer. The Drama Maker needed a job and the means to take care of himself financially. The whole family had been paying the price for the Drama Maker for over 10 years. With his wheel full, being fully supported and now being drug free, he started to apply for jobs, and, with a little interview coaching, he got a job that was physical and could enable him work out (without having to pay for gym membership) and get paid at the same time. He also now has his own apartment that he rents and is responsible for.

As you can see in this example, getting a job and being responsible is the last piece, not the first. If the Drama Maker isn't balanced, happier in themselves and supported, they won't hold a job for long, they won't be able to pay the rent, and they will spiral down again. What the family decided was a long-term 'team' approach and a plan to gently lure the Drama Maker out of his drama into his Greatness. They did this with experts, doctors, counsellors, psychologists and rehabilitation programs. It took over two years to figure it out and work it through. What makes this exciting is that people stopped 'helping' and focussed on an area to support the person they cared about.

If you know a person who is experiencing one of these patterns, and you are NOT a current Great8™ Investor, you now know where you could start being with them to help balance them out to realise their Greatness. Also note, this worked because all the family members and their support team agreed to work together to make a change: they got advice and support for the son and also for themselves. I strongly suggest you build a team for someone first, before you try and go it alone.

I just love this is. Can you tell? We no longer have to discard or write people off any more. Everyone can make a meaningful contribution to another person without over-supporting or disabling them.

Chapter 9

Helping hurts, supporting strengthens!
~ Jen Harwood

Chapter 10

How to bring a Great8™ Investor into your wheel

We've talked a lot so far about why you need Great8™ Investors in your life, what the different roles are and how to work with them. Now I want to talk about how to bring Investors into your life and into your Greatness Wheel.

Known Investor

You know them and, after thinking about who they are and what you know about them already, you know they would be great. Do the following:

1. Research first. Identify what their strengths are and how they have mastered the Domain you are focussed on: you want to be sure they have experience in in it.
2. Sometimes people aren't clear how to support you and it is best if you can guide them about the type of support you need.

3. Remember, they will get something out of this, too. If you are reluctant to ask someone you know, re-read what they get as a return on investment and the personal benefit to them on page 91.
4. Talk to them about the Greatness Principle® and/or give them a copy of this book and tell them who they are for you!
5. Share with them who your other Great8™ Investors are. Organise for them all to catch up for a dinner, lunch, conference call or meeting. It's good for them to meet likeminded people and it's good for you if they know each other.
6. Keep sharing your vision and update your progress with them.
7. Meet with them regularly, as appropriate to you both. This could be daily, weekly, monthly, bi-monthly. One of my friends in Australia talks to her Sage who lives in New Zealand and each year they plan to catch up in person in either Sydney or Auckland.

Unknown Investor

You don't know them or where to find the type of person you are looking for. Here's how to find them.

1. Tell the people in your life the role you are looking for. Ask them to be on the lookout for you and introduce you. Remember, you want Greatness. Now is not the time to be shy. You have to stop caring about looking good or being perfect. Start telling people where you need support and who you want.
2. Think about where this type of person would be hanging out: business events, the gym, mothers' clubs, golf clubs, coffee shops, the library. Wherever it is, join up and/or go hang out there. Now, this isn't stalking and following people out of a local spot wanting to talk to them. It's basic networking, and I've written a book about it that you can get, if you need it (*The Art of Networking*, 2007). Remember, like attracts like, so the best place to find a financial advisor is at a meeting about wealth creation. You could conceivably meet a financial advisor paddle-boarding at the local

beach, but it's less likely. So start in the obvious places first and be OPEN to meeting your new Grounder at your child's birthday party, your Scholar waiting for the bus, and your Enthusiast at a boring seminar where they encourage you to heckle the presenters from the back of the room! (Yes, that happened to me, I'm not going to name names ☺).

3. Say yes to parties, events and social gatherings. Where you would normally say no and not go, have the courage to show up. Sitting in the office or staying at home is not going to create Greatness. Come on, you've got a mission now—to find a Great8™ for your vision and dream.

4. At networking events or group gatherings, listen and look for the role you are looking for. For example, an Enthusiast will be encouraging, praising and be generally excited about other people. Grounders will ask lots of questions, shake their heads and tell you the problems involved. That's what they do! A Catalyst (negative) may listen to your vision/idea briefly, not pay attention fully and then say something that upsets you, angers you or makes you crazy, then walks away completely oblivious to the reaction you've just had. A Catalyst (positive) will listen to your vision/idea and will then immediately give you an introduction to a person who can open all the doors and opportunities for you or ask you directly, 'How much money do you need to make this happen?'

5. Listen to your friends. Sometimes, your friends have great people in their Great8™. Watch, listen and spend time with them to see if they too are a good fit for you. If not, they may know someone who could support you better.

The Benefits of groups

Group support can be easier than one-on-one

Groups can really work in a Great8™ role. As long as the group members are living, and you can talk with them and get corrective feedback from them, then it works! Groups are fantastic for starting to build your Greatness Wheel. For people feeling very challenged about trusting one person and building such a personal connection and being vulnerable, the group can be the Investor role all by itself. For example, when I was in massive breakdown and experiencing massive debt, relationship breakdown and my life wasn't working, I enrolled in The Landmark Forum (www.landmarkeducation.com). This is a personal development program that's run all over the world for people wanting breakthroughs in having the life that they want and a life they love.

I didn't know it at the time, but Landmark Education came into my Greatness Wheel in two roles immediately—Catalyst and Scholar. I did quite a few of their programs and I learned a lot about myself and the impact I have on others. I learned about relationships and I also started to rebuild my character and integrity to my word and values. It was a very intense two years. I was at the University of Life with them and I grew. I also found Kathy, one of my best friends and now my Anchor. Even though Kathy and I didn't grow up together, the experiences we had at Landmark Education had us so open, so raw, so trusting and vulnerable with each other that we ended up knowing each other and holding each other to fulfil our purest dreams and possibilities.

I've also done a lot of Anthony Robbins' (www.tonyrobbins.com) programs: Life Mastery®, Date with Destiny® and Unleash the Power Within®. For me, Tony's programs fitted into the Motivator and Catalyst categories. He is a master coach and a super human being, and I've watched him many times motivate and inspire people to be great (Motivator) AND he's also done many 'interventions' with audience members and participants in his programs to 'interrupt' behaviour, mindset and actions (Catalyst/Grounder). I've also met lots of people from the Tony Robbins events from all over the world, some of whom I still connect with today. They have supported me over the years in a variety of ways and I would never have met these people if I had not done these seminars and programs. You never know who you are going to meet and who can support you along the way. Diversity is brilliant, and the more people you surround yourself with who are different to you and want to support you, the better life gets.

Hobby and interest groups make us more interesting! If we are all work and family all the time, that's a bit limiting. If you collect something, like to do something, chances are there is a local special interest group such as travel, photography, scrapbooking, motorbike riding or even bushwalking. Go to these groups and be on the lookout for people you relate to as they just might be your new Great8™ for another part of your life. I've met fabulous people when I've travelled or taken up a new hobby or craft that I'm still connected to now.

For example, I met a beautiful woman 15 years ago at a Goddess Series Women's Event. I was the keynote speaker and Ganga Ashworth was the guest singer. We were talking backstage and I really liked her. She was fun, talented and professional. She taught me how to prepare my voice and calm my nerves as I was new to speaking at the time and worried at how big the space was and how I was going to project my voice into it. The event went extremely well and I have kept in contact with Ganga occasionally ever since.

It's fair to say that we have been Bystanders for each other over the years. Then, when I moved back to Sydney (where Ganga lives), our relationship and investment in each other changed. Ganga was no longer a Bystander. She moved into Sage (with my sister Kate) and Ganga was right there with me, holding my hand (and singing) at the birth of baby Rose!

If you'd told me when I'd first met Ganga backstage or in the following 10 years that we'd be having my baby 'together', I would have never imagined it, as we weren't in that realm at all. Not even close.

Chapter 10

Groups are a great place where you can invest in others

One of the strategies to finding your Great8™ is to be an Investor for someone else. Groups are good for that, as you can meet a whole bunch of new people and look for people who need the support you are prepared to give. Charity and volunteer groups are a great example of this. There are many programs that create support for people in need, such as Camp Quality, Big Brother and Big Sister Programs, Adopt a Grandparent, Meals on Wheels, LifeLine, support groups (for addictions, for illnesses, for life changes). Never underestimate the power of investing in someone else's life. It's great for them, and it's great for you!

Specific support groups are also very beneficial to start finding your Great8™ Investors as you get group information and encouragement on the subject you are there for. The other benefit of a support group is that you can take your time to listen, learn and find the people who are getting the results you want and are people you trust.

People matter and they are more than just their job, their body, their city, their house, their husband, their wife, their children, their past or even their present circumstances.
Invest in them. Love them.
~ Jen Harwood

Chapter 11

Case studies

1. Business

How a business breaks down 'overnight'

Sarah owned one of the best restaurants in town. She and her business partner, Tom, ran the business together. Their respective spouses and children loved the business too; however, they were not involved in the day-to-day business activities at all. Tom was the head chef and Sarah ran the front of house, and did all the administration and marketing. They were a dynamic combination and, from the day they took over the business, the locals came in droves for quality food and excellent customer service. The business was an established name in the community and everything was going great for everyone. Sarah's Greatness Wheel was full and it was working beautifully.

Until … one day Sarah's best friend, Lauren, told her that she was leaving town as she'd been offered a great job in London. It was an excellent and unexpected opportunity for her friend and Sarah was genuinely happy that Lauren had this great break in her career. Sarah organised the huge farewell party for friends and family and then,

Chapter 11

after Lauren left, Sarah was flat and very sad. What she didn't know at the time was that her Sage had just flown to London and was going to be out of regular contact, as Lauren would be very busy with her new life and job for at least a few months. Sarah used to talk to Lauren daily about everything. Not knowing anything about the Greatness Principle® at the time, Sarah kept going about her business and missed Lauren very much.

One day soon afterwards, Sarah was having a conversation with the local butcher. Due to market conditions, the price of meat was going up—a lot. Sarah and Tom's pricing didn't work well with that and Sarah thought that she would just have to market harder and bring in more customers. She didn't tell anyone in her Great8™ what was going on as she thought she had it handled. After a few months, it was obvious that this strategy wasn't working as she had more customers buying, and they were effectively selling meals for a loss. Their profitability dropped substantially and when it came time to pay the butcher for meat supplied, she didn't have the money. She avoided him, put him off, delayed payment, only partially paid him and then eventually changed butchers, still owing the first butcher money. She gradually got herself into the same mess with the second butcher. She'd got rid of her Catalyst and created a bigger problem.

Sarah again tried to figure it out for herself. One day, her business advisor and Scholar, David, came in for a meal and bluntly told her that the business was a mess, that she had better sort it out or it was going to be a disaster. Then he overwhelmed her with strategies on how to re-jig the menu with different types of dishes to reduce the cost of meals. Sarah was angry and felt exposed, and had a big argument with him about the quality of the brand of the business and how his strategies would kill their business, and asked him to leave.

Sarah didn't want to be told and she didn't ask for advice. She knew she had a problem. She tried all sorts of strategies to pay the bills, and eventually decided she had to let go of a few staff to make it work. So Sarah became the front of house person with one main wait person,

Pete, who was a close personal friend who needed a job, and some casual waiters for peak times. Tom, the head chef, was getting worried and didn't know what to do.

Sarah is a beautiful woman, but, as the front of house person for the restaurant seven days a week, she started to look tired. She always wore black, and she was frustrated, angry and grumpy. She no longer had time to speak to her girlfriends (Bystanders), as she was constantly working.

Sarah also wasn't being the person that was clever, witty and delightful with the regular customers, who enjoyed having Sarah saunter over, ask how their evening was going and have a meaningful conversation with them. Sarah was the one greeting guests, taking the orders, delivering the dishes and, sometimes, forgetting the little things, and snapping at the casual staff, who had no training because Sarah didn't have the time to train them. Depending on her mood or exhaustion levels, her permanent wait staff member, Pete, would be the one to pop over to the table with Sarah there and try to be a ray of sunshine in the dark, depressing cloud that Sarah was raining on the customers. The restaurant was losing its regulars (Enthusiasts) in their droves.

The cash flow of the business was bad. Tom was very concerned, and Sarah and Tom were fighting. There was no money to pay their families, and their spouses were concerned with the business position. The accountant was brought in and he declared the business was insolvent. If they closed the doors right then, they could save their houses. Sarah didn't want a bar of that. She could fix this. She told the accountant that she could fix it, and so he left the meeting, shaking his head with real concern: Grounder gone.

A few more months went by, sales dropped, the business slowed down. They no longer opened during the day, just at night for dinner. The business couldn't meet its obligations and Sarah was left standing with only one of her Great8™ left—Tom (Anchor). He sat down with her one night on the back steps and said, 'We've got to stop, Sarah, I need to get a job. The business can't pay me a wage and I can't feed my kids or pay for the house.' In that moment, Sarah realised the business was dead. Her dream was dead and she'd lost everything.

What's more incredible is that this all happened within six months.

I have seen this happen a lot over the years. You have, too. Good people doing good things suddenly fail, fall over or go broke. Have you ever heard the question, 'Why do bad things happen to good people?' Well, now you know. They lose their Great8™ Investors and they don't replace and rebuild their support network. They go into survival mode and become lone wolves. The more isolated and alone the wolves become, the more they fight for survival and become out of control (wild). They are harder to connect with and it is difficult to stop drowning. It is possible, though: it can be done with patience, commitment and rebuilding the right support around them. Don't try to support these people on your own. Do it as a team and have your Great8™ on board to support you.

2. Business leadership

How to rebuild a great business

I'd known John for a few years. I'd used his company's services and I liked who he was in the business community. John sat in my office with his head down, staring at the floor. This meeting was our first coaching session, as he wanted to see if I could help him. A lot of business owners come to me as the last chance before they throw in the towel and go get a 'proper job'.

John had little energy, he was tired and lost. He'd just told a very long story of where his business was and how he got there. The business was $200,000 behind in tax office payments, staff were leaving and going to competitors, his clients were not renewing contracts. John had suffered a heart attack three years before and that's why he had brought in a manager. Also, his wife, who worked part-time in the business as the book-keeper, was beside herself with worry as their home and assets were relying on this business to pay for their lifestyle. His turnover was around $2 million and his net profit was 9%.

I asked him who he had supporting him in his business and life and he looked up at me with shock. Then, as he thought about the answer, his face turned to frustration and then anger and he said, 'Jen, it's me. My wife helps, sort of, she complains and nags most of the time, staff don't listen, my manager doesn't have his head focussed and it's all back to ME!' To my surprise, he shouted out, 'I HATE THIS BUSINESS and I'm OVER IT!' I could safely assume that John didn't have his Great8™ wheel full. We sat there in silence for a few minutes.

I then said to him, 'John do you want to sell your business?' He looked at me and said yes. I then reached into my pocket and put one dollar on the table and said, 'I'll buy your business right here, right now for a dollar. Do you want to sell it?', and he said 'YES!' I asked him to take the dollar and we shook hands.

I said, 'Okay, I now own your business and you don't. Problem solved.' He actually looked relieved.

Then he said to me, 'You've got your work cut out for you, Jen, there's a lot to do.'

I said, 'I know. Don't worry, John, it's not your problem anymore. It's mine.'

'Yeah, right', he said.

Silence ... he was thinking and I was waiting. I knew John loved his business. He was good at running it and he'd been doing it for over 20 years. He was doing it, though, all by himself. In my opinion the heart attack (physical breakdown) should have woken him up to changing the way he ran the business and his life. It hadn't changed anything and now he was experiencing financial breakdown and, I suspected, emotional breakdown as well.

Chapter 11

After a few more minutes, John looked at me and said, 'What are you going to do with the business?'

'Oh, lots of things. I'm going to ring the tax office and get an arrangement sorted out. I'm going to make a few roles redundant. I'm going to put a marketing plan together, as this business has only relied on everyone knowing you, so now that you're not in it we need a different marketing angle. I'm going to stop some of the services this business does as they lose money and I'm also going to cut a few of the products offered, as they have low margin. I'm going to spend a bit of time with the manager as he is excellent, he's just been bored because you've been overriding him for the last two years. I can think of a whole lot more, but I believe the turnover can go to around $5 milion in the next few years and I won't have to step into it and actually "do" anything day to day. I don't have time for that.'

More silence. John squirmed in his chair. He was about to say something and then bit his lip and said nothing.

I waited a few more minutes.

Then he stood up, banged his hand on the table, leaned over and smiled at me and said, 'I could do that, I want to do that, that's great, Jen.'

'Wait a minute', I said, 'You sold the business to me and we shook hands. It's not your business. It's mine.'

He looked stunned. 'But it was for a dollar. Are you serious?'

'Yes', I said, 'You have always been your word, John. We shook hands and you did a deal.'

'Whaaat? Then let me buy it back. Here', he said, getting the dollar out of his pocket, 'I'll buy it back. I want it, let's deal.'

'Sit down, John, relax.'

He sat holding the dollar out for me to take.

I said, 'I know you can see opportunities for your business now—that's great. However, knowing them and doing them are two completely different things. If you want this business back, YOU are going to have to change. I am serious, you can't keep going the way you've been going.'

'Okay, sure, I'll change', he said as he leaned forward and held the dollar out.

'Good, then here's how you are going to buy your business back.

1. You're going to call your accountant and ask him for the up-to-date reports for the business and send them via email right now.
2. You're going to ring your doctor and find out how many hours he suggests you work a day.
3. You're going to ring your wife and tell her which night this week you are taking her out on a date.
4. You're going to ring your manager and tell him that you appreciate him working in the business and tomorrow morning you want to meet with him to find out about his ideas of making the business work.
5. You're going to ring your mate, Steve, whom you haven't seen for a few months and organise a fishing trip.'

'Sure', he said, 'I can do that.'

'Now', I said, 'You're going to do that all right now and I'm going to watch and listen as you do it.'

'Oh, right.' He looked a bit nervous.

He got out his mobile phone and started calling. His accountant answered and information was sent. He called the doctor's office and left a message. He picked Friday night as date night and rang his wife. She was sceptical. John put us on speakerphone and I spoke to her and said that if the business was going to change then John needed to change. He also needed to appreciate and honour his wife and so date nights were going to be a regular thing. You could see the smile beam through the phone. She accepted Friday night and happily hung up to organise a baby sitter.

John hesitated on the next one, his manager. 'Jen', he said, 'I was going to fire this guy. I think he's lazy.' I explained to John that he had been disempowering his manager for a very long time and it was amazing that he was still there. John's manager was very loyal, reliable and HONEST. John trusted his manager and his manager was very worthy of that trust. We needed to re-inspire, empower and train his manager. John called and the manager was so excited that John wanted to listen to his ideas, and kept thanking John for the call, that it was hard for John to hang up.

John then called Steve. Steve was having a bad morning and was glad to get a call from John. Steve's response to a fishing trip was so well received that he wanted to go the next weekend.

John hung up the phone from Steve and looked at me. He was beaming with happiness and said, 'Man, that feels so good. It's like I've just made everyone's day.' I smiled at him and said, 'John, you've just connected back into your support network. You cannot keep doing everything on your own. Can you now see that you are loved and that all of these people have your best interests at heart? Do you get that? DO you understand that all of these people care about you and have been trying to support you and you've been ignoring, dismissing, over-running, stopping and rejecting all of these people all the time?

'You think your life is so terrible because of them. It's because of you, mate! You've shut this all down and this morning, you've opened it all back up. Well done. Good for you.'

'Yes, thank you. Now can I buy my business back?'

Case studies

'Almost', I said. 'You've got to hire me to be your business coach.'

'Nice trick, Jen, you did all this just to get me to hire you!'

I stood up, went to the door, opened it and said, 'John, you can leave right now. If you think I'm doing this to sell you, you can GET OUT. I've got plenty of people wanting to work with me and I don't chase clients. You rejected my offer to support you and failed to acknowledge that I want the best for you. John, you did your usual number of not TRUSTING someone who was clearly demonstrating they can support you to greatness. This is what you do ALL the time.'

He sat there, stunned.

'You're right', he said. 'I've done this with so many people. I did this with Alan only yesterday, one of my suppliers last week. He wanted to share some strategies he thought would be good for my business. Oh no, I did this with my manager last month, I've been doing this … forever. You are so right. Jen, how do I stop this? I've got to stop this. It's exhausting and no wonder people steer clear of me. Jen, how do I stop this?'

'By realising you cannot lead your business and be great by yourself. You need to trust me. You need to trust the people around you. Your goal in the business is going to change from driving, achieving and isolating to visioning, empowering, acknowledging and honouring. It's a whole context shift and, in my experience, people need support from a variety of people to make this happen. All the people you called are your Great8™, and with them and me, you will have a GREAT business and life because you have the best support, advice, strategies and connections to make it happen.' I then shared The Greatness Principle® with him.

'Where's the coaching agreement?' he asked.

I gave it to him and after he had signed, I held out my hand. He gave me the dollar. We went to shake hands and he reached past my hand and gave me a huge hug, saying, 'Today, Jen, my life has just changed forever and I can't thank you enough.' (I love it when this happens with clients!)

'Consider your business sold back to you, John. It's all yours just as it is and YOU have everything you need and the right support to change it and make it work for you, your family, your staff, suppliers and the community we serve.'

After that conversation, John's business grew at an awesome rate. He did all the things I suggested and more. Three years later, all the debt was repaid and he had leveraged the business to create assets and superannuation and had cleared personal mortgages. John sold the business to his manager five years after we met. John now mentors his manager about running and growing the business as he is his manager's Scholar. John no longer disposes of relationships and people: he trusts, he listens more than he talks and he's told me that he loves his wife even more than when they first met. This is a very different place to when we first met five years earlier. John did the work of reconnecting and rebuilding his support network and by doing that he changed his entire point of view about his life and his business. That is what the Greatness Principle® is all about.

3. Career

Broke, drunk and depressed

Dave had everything he wanted in life. He had a wife who loved him (Grounder), children who loved him (Enthusiasts), a comfortable home, a nice car and a job that he enjoyed working at. He had solid mates: Rob, who'd worked with him in the past, would get on his back and hold him accountable (Motivator), and Shaun, whom Dave had known for years and they had been best men at each other's wedding (Sage).

Dave was a consultant. He was a succession strategist working with long-running companies, who assisted business owners to transition out of business by either handing it over to the owners' children, selling to staff, or selling the entire business. Dave had been working with one particular client for nearly two years. He was part of the senior management of the business and was making a big contribution to the owners in the areas of goals, direction leadership and junior management training.

Dave really enjoyed working with this company for a number of reasons. The owners were in the same age bracket as Dave (Bystanders). The younger staff (Scholars) were great to be with, as they kept asking questions and demanding training and learning. Dave kept studying and learning to keep up to speed so he could be of value to them. Also, for Dave to be effective in this business transition, he did a lot of networking in the industry, getting to know other business owners, leaders, consultants and a wide variety of people to enable him to understand the industry his client was in.

Dave's life was pretty great. He was, however, missing a vital Great8™ Investor, the Anchor. His brother had died a few years earlier. It was a very sad story and the loss of Dave's brother rippled throughout the entire family; however, it really affected Dave and he didn't really know how much the loss had affected his life. The challenge that Dave had was that his confidence was very low. The Anchor is a vital relationship that nurtures and builds your confidence. Dave had been missing his Anchor for about five years. Still, with seven out of eight Investors, you can have a good to great life, and Dave did.

Dave loved his client and the work he was doing. He was being effective, and that by itself kept his confidence high. He was planning to be with this company for another 18 months to fulfil the contract, so he didn't do much business development or marketing because he only worked with one company at a time. Then one day, out of the blue, his client received an offer to be bought out by the largest player in the industry. It was a very, very good deal for the business owners and it would enable the owners to make sure all of their 80 staff had jobs to go to after the buyout was done. Dave was happy for the client and supported everyone to be ready. The sale was taking place in three months. This was going to have a big impact on Dave, and he didn't even know it.

Three months later, the business was sold, the deal was done and Dave's mission was accomplished, albeit early. Dave went to the celebration drinks, and it was a happy day. The next morning, Dave woke up and realised that he didn't have anything to do. There was no new work on the horizon. Dave stayed at home, went for coffee and read the paper and spent time talking to the neighbours. He wasn't doing anything productive and soon his wife (Grounder) started talking about getting a new contract, a new job or something to bring in money. Dave was relaxed as there were some savings, so he took his time. He'd worked hard these last few years: he didn't need to rush.

Dave was not motivated at all. Due to the sale of the business and contract ending, Dave had instantly lost his Bystander and Scholar. He was down to five Investors. Also at this time, his eldest son, aged 26, whom he'd go to the gym with (Motivator), got a new girlfriend and with the change in priorities didn't want to go to the gym with Dave after work. So now Dave effectively had four in his wheel and he was at home, alone, during the day. He didn't like this and he didn't know what to do about it.

He'd tinker around on his computer, build his LinkedIn profile and apply online for jobs. Nothing was doing it for him. He was lost. So he did what he loved to do … he went and sat in a cafe and read the paper, talked to strangers and connected with as many people as possible. Pretty soon it wasn't just cafes he frequented: he went to bars and pubs. He started being out all day and coming home late at night. Due to the new activity, he wasn't spending quality time with his wife and kids, and coming home drunk wasn't adding to their relationship. It was damaging it.

Several months of this behaviour continued and Dave was nowhere closer to finding a job. The savings he'd put aside were almost gone and the drinking and abusive behaviour were getting more often and worse. One afternoon, he came home to find his wife had moved all her stuff out. She had had enough of his behaviour and told him that she couldn't live with him being so self-destructive. She told him he needed to clean up his act, get a job and start respecting himself and her and the children. (Grounder and Enthusiasts gone). Dave was devastated. He had no money, the house they were renting was let go, all his stuff went into storage (which he couldn't afford), and he didn't have anywhere to live and no money to pay for it. He had his phone and mobile tablet and, for the first few weeks, he lived out of his car and a mate's place on the couch. Dave was in total breakdown and it didn't look good.

Dave was totally ashamed of his situation and didn't talk to anyone about it. He avoided his friends' calls. He borrowed money from acquaintances so he could drink and wallow. Dave was a very charming, smooth-talking man. People liked him, which made it even harder for him to admit he had a problem and that his life was going backwards.

Luckily for Dave his mate Rob (Motivator) went out of his way to come and see him. Dave told Rob everything. There were lots of tears, as Dave was in total despair. Rob got Dave to start creating the vision of how Dave wanted his life to be. He got Dave to connect to his top priorities and focussed him on actions that would make it happen. Rob was direct, uplifting and straight. If you're going to make something happen, the Motivator is the perfect Investor to be kicking you and pushing you.

In this conversation, Dave woke up. His top priority was getting back with his wife. To do that, he needed to demonstrate that he was reliable and had a job. The pressure that she was under to do everything with her job and the children by herself was a heavy burden. She was stoic and strong, yet he hated that he'd put her in that position in the first place. He stopped drinking as much, began using his smartphone to apply for jobs and start changing his life. Dave was taking responsibility for his life and Rob called him almost daily to make sure Dave was in action.

After eight weeks of activity, Dave had an interview for a job that suited his skills and personality. He told his wife that he had this particular interview and she was genuinely happy for him. She listened and encouraged his preparation and supported him with some money to put fuel in the car so he could drive to the interview. She wanted him to be working. She wanted him to be Great. A new job was essential for him to manage himself and also contribute financially to her and the children.

To everyone's relief, Dave was offered the job and he accepted it. What was great about this new job was that there were strong, successful business people there who were going to be Dave's manager, colleagues and support. In this new role, Dave automatically gained Mark (Anchor), his new manager. Mark was the one in Dave's interview who saw his potential and could see he would be a long-term asset to the company. He also gained several Scholars, Bystanders, Catalysts, Motivators and a Sage, who was the owner of the business. This job role filled Dave's wheel and almost doubled every role almost overnight and, as a result, Dave started to grow and learn at a rapid rate.

At the time of writing, Dave still works for this company and he's one of the top performers. He's living back with his wife and kids, and he's happier about who he is and what he's doing. He's managing his emotions better. His wife is happier. Life for Dave is not perfect, yet compared to where he was, life is great and he's working on it to be even better.

4. Spiritual enlightenment

The role of God or a higher power in the greatness
Okay, for the lone wolves out there and those who think I might be preaching in this next bit, relax. I'm not going to try to convert you

to do or believe anything. If you think I am, or have a secret agenda, truly I don't. Just treat me in this section as your Catalyst.

In 2009, I was still in Bendigo and my life was going great. I had my Great8™ Investors in place. I was out of financial debt, I'd bought a house and my very first brand new Mercedes Benz. My mum was doing much better, Dad was great, I had solid relationships with girlfriends, my accountant, my best friends scattered across the country and, I'm happy to say, my Great8™ wheel was very full. (By the way, you don't need a life partner/spouse to have a full wheel and a great life.)

What you don't know is that I had been on a spiritual quest for a long time, and one day I signed up a new client, Michelle. Michelle was inventing a new product and needed support and guidance on how to set up a business, raise capital and get the project moving. She'd never done anything like this before and she 'just knew' I was the person to get her started and on the right track. We had lots of great coaching sessions and she was in action and getting results. As I got to know Michelle, I met her husband, Greg. My relationship with them both got more personal and deeper. The more we got together outside of business coaching, the more we talked about life. They had been married for over 20 years and endured challenges between them, with their children and even in the community. Having been divorced at 30 and been single for the last eight years, I wanted to learn the secret to their relationship, as, having seen the results my top clients were getting in life, I was still on a quest to learn more about having long-term relationships. So I adopted them into my life 'unofficially' into the Domain of marriage as my Scholars.

It came out in conversation one day that they were Christians and that they truly lived a life of love, prayer, forgiveness, worship and service. After spending a few more months with Michelle working on her business, I noticed that Michelle had an excitement, pure joy and total certainty when we were talking about the future and the unknown of what she needed to do in her business. When I asked her why she was so excited, joyful and certain that everything would happen (as most of my clients were scared, uncertain and needed courage to take the next step), Michelle's answer was, 'Jen, God is my business partner!'

Whaaat? I thought I'd heard everything from clients, and yet I hadn't heard this one before. After thinking for a brief moment that she was crazy, and that I really didn't know who she was any more, I realised that she was dead serious and that I was about to learn something. So I leaned in and started to really listen to her as she described her relationship with God. She beamed a brilliant smile that went from ear to ear as she told me that she talked with God, lived and walked with God, and trusted God completely with all of her heart. God was in her life and her marriage, and surrounded her whole human experience. It was quite profound being with her as the excitement, energy and conviction intensified as she talked. It was amazing. She was so deliriously happy and content with this relationship. I've only felt deliriously happy and content for a few minutes at a time, when I eat an amazing chocolate or climax in orgasm. Michelle was living in that experience, daily. It was hard to take in and believe.

Upon reflection, Michelle had her Great8™ wheel full in a number of Domains—marriage, family, community, church—and she was working with me on business/career. I must admit that I resisted and ignored Michelle's comments for a few more meetings until one day, when she was yet again oozing possibility, faith and belief about being supported in her business and future challenges, I burst out with, 'Michelle, I want the relationship you have with God too. How do I get that?' She screamed with delight, grabbed me and squashed me with a passionate hug, and said, 'It's easy.'

We bowed our heads and she said a long prayer. As she did this, the top of my head got very warm and then that warmth ran down my spine and all through my body. I felt so loved, so peaceful and so very grateful. It was an incredible experience and we were both in tears at the end. I don't really know what happened physically. What I do know is that I surrendered to life and everything that is, that I recognised that my life is about me and yet it's not about me at all. I got that I'm not alone, I never was, and that's when I totally surrendered my ego, judgements, projections, fear, constraints and limitations. I am still loved and life will and does work even better knowing this.

So now, reflecting on my whole life, and knowing the Greatness Principle® and how it works, in all of the times I've ever achieved anything great, whether it be winning academic, business or sporting awards, completing a major business project, raising capital for clients, writing and launching my first book, or down to the day-to-day great achievements such as finding the perfect home to live in, creating the best holiday ever or loving and supporting my parents while my mother was terminally ill, I did all of these things with the investment and contribution of great people around me. I didn't do it by myself. I allowed others to contribute to me with ideas, strategies, encouragement, accountability, motivation, reality, excitement and gentle nudges to believe in possibility. Yes, I committed to an inspiring vision and then surrendered myself to people I trusted and the result was awesome.

I've personally experienced that God/a higher power/magic is fully present when your wheel is full. What I have learned over the last few years of consciously working the Greatness Principle® is that, by surrendering to a compelling vision and trusting people to create it with you, you are learning to love and trust more and, in turn, you are letting God work with you through the people you have engaged in your Great8™. On the flip side, when things are really bad, situations and circumstances are rough and challenging, the Greatness Principle® is a way of focussing on letting people support you, encourage you, lift you and remind you about who you really are and that you are deeply loved and you have the strength, courage and determination to get through the tough times. God can and will work with you through the Great8™ Investors that you allow in.

5. Living responsibly

It's not about ME anymore
The final case study that's worth sharing with you is one that enabled me to fully understand how the Greatness Principle® works and how we can really live great lives, with and through other people. We can actually have another environmental impact on the planet—that is, reducing our 'emotional and social damage' blueprint on this earth!

I had been living in Bendigo for over five and a half years and the move from Sydney had caused huge social isolation for me that I hadn't really overcome. I hadn't grown up in Bendigo, so it was taking quite a while to find my social groups and personal support networks outside of business.

I didn't like how cold Bendigo got in the winter. I also was over the fact that Mum was still sick and living with cancer, yet at that time, she was well enough to travel, go to a movie and do lots of 'normal' things. She didn't present like she was dying—which was hard to mentally process as about nine months previously she had been admitted to a hospice as she was definitely on her way out of this world. This unpredictability and uncertainty was emotionally and mentally taxing.

I was working a LOT: I was coaching, speaking and travelling all the time and there was a big pull coming for me to move back to Sydney where I LOVED to be. My huge Mosman Bay painting that I'd bought some 10 years ago was hanging prominently in my Bendigo home as the promise, the dream, of one day I would get back to living and working next to Sydney Harbour. I missed my Sydney friends and I missed the lifestyle I had there. I didn't want the drought that the Bendigo region had been enduring for the previous five years. I didn't want to deal with death and dying anymore. I was tired, lonely and wanting more sunshine and joy in my life.

After many conversations with my Great8™, we all agreed that it looked like the right time for me to relocate. So, when I went to my parents' place for dinner for our weekly catch-up, I told them that I was planning to hand over my clients to a local coach, or convert them to other services I had on offer, rent my house out, have a garage sale and move back to Sydney. They both had their heads down eating their food and then Mum said in a low, calm voice, 'Wow, okay Jen, if that's what you really want.'

That was it, they didn't say anything more and the conversation changed to something else. I thought, great, they're not talking me out of it, so it must be the right thing to do. So after a great evening with them I went home and started to get organised and got into my week of work and life.

Two days later, on Saturday morning, there was a knock on my door. Mum and Dad were there with a litre of milk and some home-baked scones. Due to my busy lifestyle at the time, they had learned that if they wanted a cup of tea or coffee during their visit, they had to bring the milk and cakes themselves, as I didn't go shopping much and couldn't be relied upon to have supplies!

I was surprised to see them. Mum didn't get up and out of the house very often, so I raced to the door and ushered them to the kitchen where Mum promptly sat down at the kitchen table and Dad proceeded to make morning tea for us all. When he brought the mugs and warm scones to the table, I took one and before I took a bite said, 'Okay, so what's up?'

Mum said, 'Your father and I have something to ask you.'

I was intrigued and my mind raced to all the possible things they needed me to do for them that I would eagerly say yes to.

'Okay, go for it,' I said as I turned to Dad. He looked me directly and said, 'We don't want you to leave Bendigo. Would you please stay?'

Whoa! That was HUGE. Now what you don't know about my parents and how we grew up is that we were always told by our parents that

Chapter 11

we could be, do or have anything. Our parents never stopped us living our lives fully and always stood back and allowed us to make our own choices and supported us in those choices, whether they be good ones or bad ones.

So, for both of them to come to my house, to ask me NOT to do what I had decided to do, was HUGE. I must say, I was a bit shocked. My face must have shown that as Mum said, 'Jen, you've been so great with both of us and you moving to Bendigo has been so wonderful for us all to be so close. We know what we are asking and we will let you decide for yourself. We love you no matter what you choose.'

I said, 'Okay, can you let me think about it?' They said of course and after a few more minutes, Dad packed up the kitchen, left the milk and scones and escorted Mum back to the car. What had just happened? I was confused and very curious.

I couldn't run fast enough to my office and get to my huge whiteboard. I drew two Greatness Wheels, one for Mum and one for Dad. I had a feeling I was going to discover something, I just didn't know what.

Mum's wheel was quite full. She had seven out of her eight—okay, all good there. Then I did Dad's wheel and as I started to look at his life and the meaningful, intimate relationships he had, I realised that there had actually been quite a lot of change for him in the last six months. One of the men that he had caught up with to talk about politics, religion and life had died. The other had been put into a nursing home. Due to Mum's illness and her nearly dying twice in the last year, Dad had been over-supporting Mum and even though her wheel was almost full, Dad hadn't gone back to his life to regain new support. Worryingly, Dad only had four in his wheel, and I realised that if I left and moved to Sydney **at that point in time**, Dad would go into breakdown: in fact, he was on the edge of it already. I'm certain that Mum and Dad felt this about Dad, but couldn't articulate it, as they didn't know about the Greatness Principle® in as much detail as we do now.

In that moment, I realised that my life just isn't about ME. I have an impact on others, whether I consciously choose it or not. I was Dad's Enthusiast. Every time I came back from a speaking engagement, I'd tell him all about it. I'd then take an active interest in what he was doing, what he was writing about and generally the world of Bob. We would have heaps of fun sharing stories of his past working days and my current work adventures. I was an excellent distraction from dealing with cancer and death for him. I lived in the world of possibility, wonder, energy and excitement. He loved it. I loved sharing it with him and I was, and still am, Bob's Enthusiast.

I realised that, before I could go anywhere, I needed to support Dad in rebuilding his Greatness Wheel. I remembered one of my great mentors at Landmark Education saying to me, 'Jen, if you can't deliver, don't complain, or ignore it. It's your responsibility to replace yourself.' That is what I had to do with Bob: replace the Enthusiast role I filled and find three to four people for the other Great8™ who Bob could spend time with.

I drove over to my parents' house that afternoon. It was a lovely sunny, warm afternoon. Mum was in the back garden on a reclining deck lounge resting, and Dad was deep in the back garden with his veggies. I went up to Mum and gave her a kiss. I said to her, 'I'll go and get Dad.' She nodded and smiled a knowing mother, wise old Sage smile. She knew I'd got it.

Dad saw me coming down the back path and said, 'Oh look, it's our Jennifer, two visits in one day. How lucky are we?', and gave me a hug and a kiss.

'To what do we owe the pleasure, my darling?' he asked.

I took his hand and walked with him back to Mum's chair. When we got there, I said to them both, 'What you asked me this morning was a surprise and a shock. You've never stopped me doing anything in my life until today. I've thought about your request and I want you to

Chapter 11

know, that you, my father, need me right now and I'm going to support you and Mum until that is no longer required.'

Tears welled in Bob's eyes. He looked down at his feet and said quietly, 'Thank you, Jen'.

I moved closer to him, put my arms around him and gave him a strong, loving, beautiful hug, and as I rested my head on his shoulder, I whispered in his ear, 'Bob, you need balance.'

He pulled back ever so slightly from me, and when I saw his face, he was smiling at Cath and he said softly …

'Balance would be Great!'

After thoughts ...

Being a lone wolf, surviving life and scavenging around for just enough is exhausting, frustrating and incredibly limiting. In a world that is more 'technically connected' and geographically connected than ever before, we must still connect in person. We must touch, talk and engage others with all the senses and BE with each other. Looking another human being in the eye gets to the heart of any matter in moments. People need to be heard, appreciated and 'got', and the only way to do that is through personal connection—in relationship, not in isolation.

It's time to stop doing the ME, ME, ME game and start being great WITH and FOR others.

When we go for greatness, we choose:

- to love our life fully;
- to love and appreciate the people around us;
- to accept the change and continual challenges in our life; and
- to realise our own and others' full potential.

When you have your Greatness Wheel full, in any domain of life, you get a new sense of power, confidence and possibility that didn't exist before. It's happened to me a lot and I've seen it happen with all of

After thoughts ...

my clients. They get more confidence, and in turn get more support. They start making better choices and that creates more consistency. They then get more certainty, which creates more balance, and then when the Greatness Wheel gets filled with the last Great8™ Investor, they suddenly turbocharge into their Domain of life and things are working. It's like they are 10 feet tall and bulletproof. They are on a mission to fulfil their vision and nothing is going to stop them. That is what creates success. That is what causes the greats to be great and what's exciting is that anyone can do it.

When your Great8™ wheel is full, you are balanced and you are centred.

When you are centred, you can listen.
When you listen, you can hear the sounds of life.
When you hear the sounds of life, you can feel love.
When you feel love, you are loved and ...
Everything is you
And you are everything.

Go be GREAT, because you can!

An Invitation

If you've enjoyed this book, would you like some more?

Join me online!

www.greatnessprinciple.com
www.facebook.com/greatnessprinciple
www.pinterest.com/harwood0643/the-greatness-principle
www.facebook.com/iamjenharwood
www.twitter.com/iamjenharwood
www.linkedin.com/in/jenharwood

Further Training and Courses in the Greatness Principle®

Level 1: The Great Life (2 days)

Come and do the work with me in a weekend two-day event. We will get your vision sorted, your values clear and have you connected and inspired as to what's possible for you. Then on the second day you will create your Greatness Wheel, identify the blocks and limitations in your path for asking for and receiving support, and so much more. This weekend will change your life and get you on the path to Greatness.

Level 2: The Great Leader (2 days)

Having done Level 1, The Great Life, you are now clear about your own vision and direction. When leaders are clear about what they personally want, they can attract and lead a team powerfully to create anything with them. This two-day event is designed for leaders to look at their business, company or project and 'get real' about its success. You will review or renew your vision and start to understand and appreciate what you have done to create the results you are currently getting. You will also create a plan to move forward and identify who and what the business, company or project needs to be GREAT. This is a powerful weekend where you will clear the past, get focussed on the future and, in a centred and balanced way, start to move forward with the right support to realise your vision and dreams.

The Greatness Principle® Accredited Facilitators Program (3 Days)

The prerequisite for this program is Levels 1 and 2. The reason for this is that I'm interested in all our accredited coaches, trainers and facilitators using and applying the Greatness Principle® in their life and their business. Your business must be growing, profitable and successful. Too many times I've seen accredited people being great at teaching but not run a profitable, successful business. When you come on board with us, you will learn the Greatness Principle® at a whole new level AND be able to apply it to your own business so that you will be walking the talk with your clients. You will able to demonstrate that you are great at growing, leading and managing your own business and life. This program is awesome for coaches, consultants, counsellors, social workers and therapists as well as leaders and CEOs who want a deeper understanding of how to grow and support leaders in their greatness.

An Invitation

The Greatness Principle® Coaching Programs

If you are the kind of person who prefers to receive this kind of training online, we would love you to join us for our brand new online coaching program. Including the five wheel dynamics, the top seven causes of the breakdown of The Greatness Principle®, audio versions of the amazing content from the book and so much more, I encourage you to log on now to www.greatnessprinciple.com and register for the free preview to this invaluable program.

The Greatness Principle® Products

All these products and more are available at our website www.greatnessprinciple.com.

Greatness Cards

These inspiring cards are designed to support you when you feel stuck, unsure, overwhelmed, a bit lost, or you feel that you are withdrawing from the people around you. They will gently guide you to embrace and awaken your Greatness. Filled with insight and awareness, these cards will encourage you to focus, reconnect and take action.

An Invitation

Greatness Principle® T-Shirts

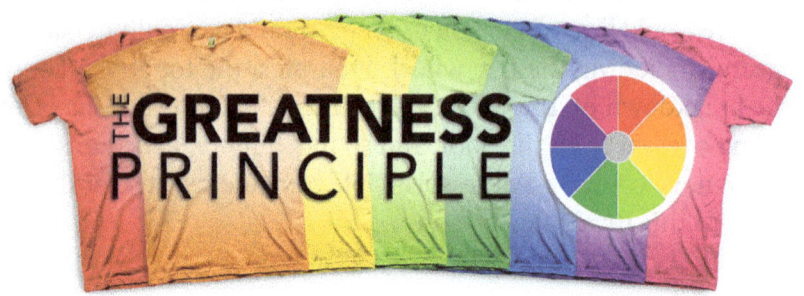

Choose from the range of T-Shirts with each of the Great8™ Investors on them.

There is also the First Investor T-Shirt, which is for you!

Rainbow Packs are available with all the shirts in them.

Greatness Party Pack

Celebrate the people who support you and throw a party when you have realised your vision. Enclosed are:

Rainbow pack of the Great8™ shirts and caps.

A certificate for each of your Great8™ for their contribution.

Special celebration activities for you to use at your party.

Imagine celebrating and acknowledging the people who have supported you to be Great! Savour that moment in time where you can all stand together and admire that you collectively caused GREAT results. A Greatness Party is worth doing for everyone. When you've had your party, post it on our Facebook and Pinterest pages. We'd love to acknowledge and share your success.

Who is Jen Harwood?

Jen grew up on an orange orchard by the side of a river in the small country town of Berri, South Australia. She grew up in a family of four children. Her parents, family and country influence created the foundation core beliefs that Jen has and lives her life by:

- Life is an adventure.
- Anything is possible and I can do anything I put my mind to.
- My job is to be the best I can be.
- My family is my number one asset.
- I love, honour, and respect the people I love.
- I love everyone, even when it's hard to find something to love in them.
- I am here to serve.
- The earth is one country and mankind its citizens.
- God is in our hearts and is with us always.

Jen's Qualifications and Awards

Batchelor of Science, 1992, University of New South Wales, Sydney, Australia.

Certified Business Coach, 2003, CoachU, USA.

Coached thousands of small business owners to grow their business and be successful leaders in just about every industry in Australia, New Zealand, Thailand, China and the United States, 1999–present

Inaugural Kerry Nairn Scholar for Professional Speaking, 2006.

Future Leader of Australia Award, DAVOS Foundation, 2008.

Certified Speaking Professional (CSP), 2009, National Speaking Association of Australia.

Jen's personal mission is **Families and Business working together to create peace and profit!** If every business / family can get the support and strategies they need to work together and flourish, everyone benefits.

Acknowledgements

Thanks to My Great8™ Investors for bringing the Greatness Principle® to life.

Enthusiast: Jen Picknell, Graphic Designer and Jenious! Louise and Mark Mulqueen who have been my cheer squad ever since we met. Thank you both for your encouragement, listening and support. Craig and Leonie—two very super excited people who encouraged me along and germinated even more possibility in this project.

Sage: My father Bob, my sister Kate and my grandmother Polly. Your love, support and wisdom through the recent challenges of my life and marriage have really supported me to hold the space, be true to my values and honour my family. Thank you. Also thanks to Suzy— thank you for taking care of our baby Rose. Your silent strength and commitment to our family was small in time yet huge in impact.

Motivator: Kylee Legge, the Publishing Queen. You are the best Motivator I've met in a very long time. Thank you for whipping me and this project into shape!

Bystander: All of my past clients and friends who have been hearing me talk about this for years. Especially, Greg Hearn, Clare Fountain,

Acknowledgements

Gary and Toni-Marie Carter, Bev Barnfather, Julie Crockett and Jennifer Franklin Bell.

Anchor: the people who pre-ordered the book over four years ago.

Specific thanks to 11 key people: I started speaking about the Greatness Principle®, then known as The First Investor Principle, in late 2009 in Yarrawonga, a small town in Central Victoria in Australia. It was my maiden speech on the topic and, being excited and certain that I could easily create and write my next book within 3–4 months like I did the previous book I had written, *The Art of Networking* (which sold 5000 copies), I offered the option for people to pre-order a copy.

Well, these 11 people put their money down and have patiently waited four years to see this book come to light. I am so sorry to have kept them waiting AND I am so grateful that they pre-ordered and paid for the book because, if they had not, I probably wouldn't have pursued this project. I could have easily given up due to all the 'stuff' that was happening in my life and just refunded their money, which I thought about doing several times.

However, the event I spoke at in Yarrawonga was an amazing event. At the end of the presentation, in those seconds between the audience knowing you'd finished and before the applause, the room was completely silent, they were soaking it in and processing in their minds the impact of what they had just heard. I watched them, they were moved, and two people were crying. I privately asked them afterwards why they were in tears and one had realised why her business had failed and the other had understood why his marriage had ended. WOW!

I've never forgotten that presentation, the people in it and the experience we had. That has been my Anchor for the Greatness Principle®. We should all be so grateful that these people were the first investors into this project and, because of them, it now has the ability to make a difference and touch so many people's lives so deeply. To you all ... Phil Chamberlain, Kathryn Dalitz, Lyn Haynes, Mark Magill, Mike Dove, Jenny Cox, Penne Tregenzo, Robin Cobb, Damien Hipwell, Andrew Brown, Jan Barned, Vanessa Bennet... I sincerely thank you for your investment and faith in the Greatness Principle® and am so grateful for your patience in waiting so long to get it.

Grounder: My daughter Rose—you are my motivation to be as GREAT as I can. Simon—thank you for allowing me to share our stories. Also special thanks to my editor Gaye Wilson—I'm touched to my core that you 'got' my message and have made it even better.

Catalyst: Christine Silvestroni and Enterprise Geelong, for giving us a launch date and venue. Chris, thank you for your belief and commitment to making the world a better place. You are an extraordinary person.

Also special thanks to the financial investors who catalysed this business being launched!

Financial Investors:

To my friends Kim, Belle, Bob, Louise, Meegan, Sophie, Bev, Tim, Kathy, Greg, Jennifer, David and Michael, thank you for believing in me and putting your money on the table!

The clients who have also invested in me that I'm delighted to promote include:

Gary Carter, Eagle Training Services, Alice Springs, NT
www.eagletraining.com.au

Liz Valek, Clover Fields, Sydney, NSW
www.cloverfields.com

Acknowledgements

Your investment gave this project such a surge and drive that made it possible for us to hit the turbo button. Thank you so much.

Scholar: National Speakers Association of Australia and fellow CSPs including Allan Parker, Catherine Palin-Brinkworth, Matt Church and Lou Heckler.

Thank you to all the clients I have worked with over the past 15 years that have taught me so much and enabled me to create this work. Thank you for trusting me with your businesses, family and personal world. To coach is a humbling experience and a true honour. Your vulnerability and trust has enabled me to support so many more, thank you.

Inspiration: Finally, I'd like to thank my mother, Cath. She knew all about the Greatness Principle® as we talked about it a lot when she was alive. Cath was my Sage and now she's my inspiration to live life to the fullest, to teach people how to love and support each other, and to be the best human being I can be every day in every way, no matter what the circumstances.

God Bless

Jen

Greatness Wheel templates

It's a great idea to keep this book and come back to it over time to see how you are tracking and the adjustments you need to make. For more copies of the wheel you can download them anytime from our website: www.greatnessprinciple.com.

Name	
Domain	
Date	

SPIRIT

▼ ENTHUSIAST   ▼ SAGE

▶ SCHOLAR   ▼ MOTIVATOR

MIND   EMOTION

▶ CATALYST   ▼ BYSTANDER

▲ GROUNDER   ▶ ANCHOR

BODY

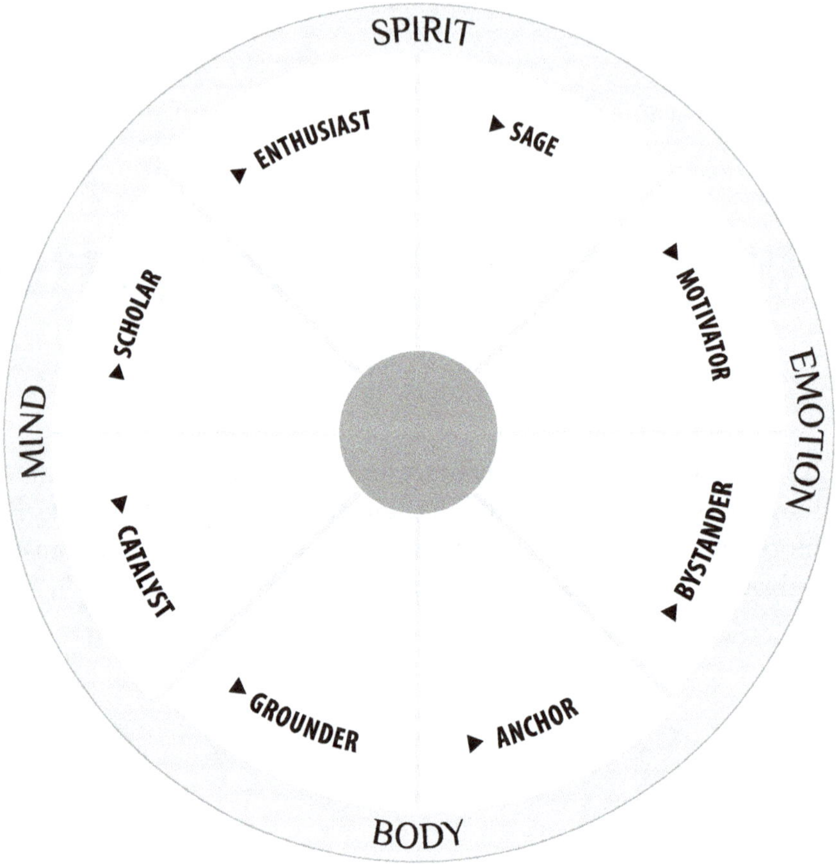

Describe what's happening right now:
_____
_____

What is your vision for this domain:
_____
_____

Actions to take to make it happen:
_____
_____

Copyright © 2014 Jen Harwood
www.greatnessprinciple.com

Name	
Domain	
Date	

SPIRIT

▸ ENTHUSIAST   ▸ SAGE

▸ SCHOLAR   ▸ MOTIVATOR

MIND   EMOTION

▸ CATALYST   ▸ BYSTANDER

▸ GROUNDER   ▸ ANCHOR

BODY

Describe what's happening right now:
_____
_____

What is your vision for this domain:
_____
_____

Actions to take to make it happen:
_____
_____

Copyright © 2014 Jen Harwood
www.greatnessprinciple.com

Name	
Domain	
Date	

SPIRIT

▲ ENTHUSIAST ▲ SAGE

▲ SCHOLAR

▲ MOTIVATOR

MIND

EMOTION

▲ CATALYST

▲ BYSTANDER

▲ GROUNDER ▲ ANCHOR

BODY

Describe what's happening right now:

What is your vision for this domain:

Actions to take to make it happen:

Copyright © 2014 Jen Harwood
www.greatnessprinciple.com

Name	
Domain	
Date	

SPIRIT

▼ ENTHUSIAST   ▼ SAGE

▶ SCHOLAR

▼ MOTIVATOR

MIND

EMOTION

▼ CATALYST

▶ BYSTANDER

▶ GROUNDER   ▶ ANCHOR

BODY

Describe what's happening right now:

What is your vision for this domain:

Actions to take to make it happen:

Copyright © 2014 Jen Harwood
www.greatnessprinciple.com

Name:

Domain:

Date:

SPIRIT

- ▶ ENTHUSIAST
- ▶ SAGE
- ▶ SCHOLAR
- ▶ MOTIVATOR
- ▶ CATALYST
- ▶ BYSTANDER
- ▶ GROUNDER
- ▶ ANCHOR

MIND

EMOTION

BODY

Describe what's happening right now:

What is your vision for this domain:

Actions to take to make it happen:

Copyright © 2014 Jen Harwood
www.greatnessprinciple.com

Name	
Domain	
Date	

SPIRIT

▸ ENTHUSIAST ▸ SAGE

▸ SCHOLAR

▸ MOTIVATOR

MIND

EMOTION

▸ CATALYST

▸ BYSTANDER

▸ GROUNDER ▸ ANCHOR

BODY

Describe what's happening right now:

What is your vision for this domain:

Actions to take to make it happen:

Copyright © 2014 Jen Harwood
www.greatnessprinciple.com

Name	
Domain	
Date	

SPIRIT

▼ ENTHUSIAST   ▼ SAGE

▶ SCHOLAR   ▼ MOTIVATOR

MIND   EMOTION

▶ CATALYST   ▼ BYSTANDER

▲ GROUNDER   ▶ ANCHOR

BODY

Describe what's happening right now:
_____
_____

What is your vision for this domain:
_____
_____

Actions to take to make it happen:
_____
_____

Copyright © 2014 Jen Harwood
www.greatnessprinciple.com

Name	
Domain	
Date	

SPIRIT

▼ ENTHUSIAST ▼ SAGE

▶ SCHOLAR

MIND ▶ MOTIVATOR **EMOTION**

◀ CATALYST ◀ BYSTANDER

▲ GROUNDER ▶ ANCHOR

BODY

Describe what's happening right now:
_____
_____

What is your vision for this domain:
_____
_____

Actions to take to make it happen:
_____
_____

Copyright © 2014 Jen Harwood
www.greatnessprinciple.com

Name	
Domain	
Date	

SPIRIT

ENTHUSIAST ▸ SAGE

▸ MOTIVATOR

MIND ▸ SCHOLAR

EMOTION

▸ BYSTANDER

▸ CATALYST

▸ GROUNDER ▸ ANCHOR

BODY

Describe what's happening right now:

What is your vision for this domain:

Actions to take to make it happen:

Copyright © 2014 Jen Harwood
www.greatnessprinciple.com

Name	
Domain	
Date	

SPIRIT

▼ ENTHUSIAST   ▼ SAGE

▲ SCHOLAR   ◀ MOTIVATOR

MIND   EMOTION

◀ CATALYST   ▶ BYSTANDER

▲ GROUNDER   ▶ ANCHOR

BODY

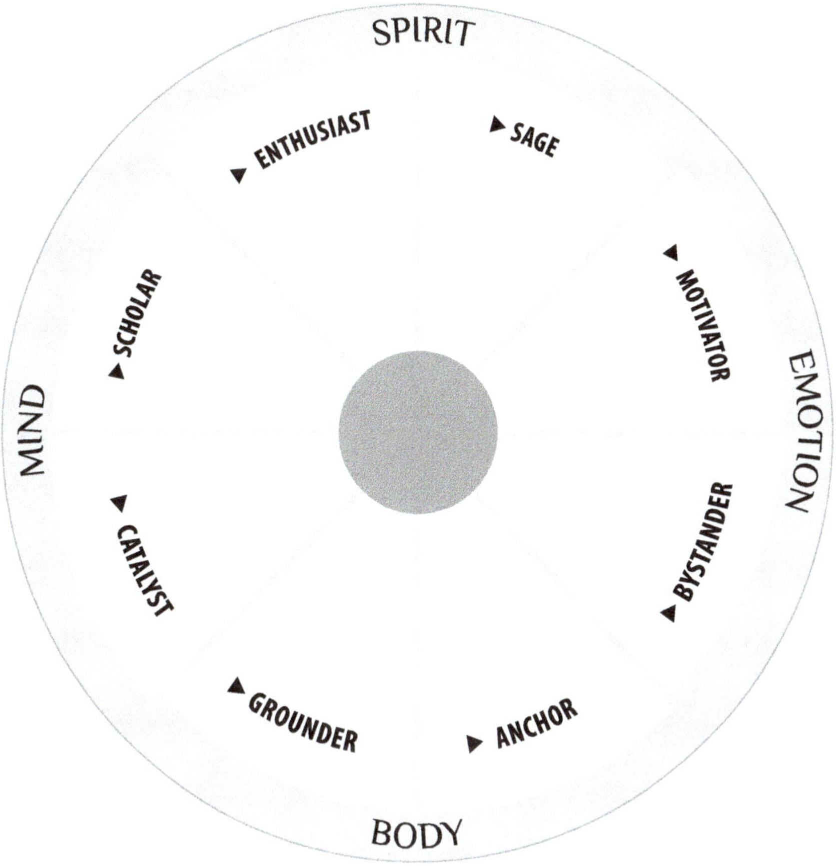

Describe what's happening right now:

What is your vision for this domain:

Actions to take to make it happen:

Copyright © 2014 Jen Harwood
www.greatnessprinciple.com

www.ingramcontent.com/pod-product-compliance
Lightning Source LLC
Chambersburg PA
CBHW050122020526
44112CB00035B/2283